The Eight *Callings* Of God

Dr. Ted Traylor

Lakewood Ranch, Florida

By Dr. Ted Traylor

Published by Outcome Publishing
11523 Palm Brush Trail #372
Bradenton, Florida 34202
www.outcomepublishing.com

Edited by Angie Kiesling

Cover Design by Lee Ann Martin

First Edition

Printed in the United States of America

1. Religion: Spirituality General
2. Self-Help: Spiritual
3. Religion: Christian Life – Personal Growth

Dedicated to Jean Traylor

When I was called to preach at seventeen, she purchased my first sermon preparation book for me. She exhorted me to be a good student. Thanks, Mom, for all the encouragement.

Acknowledgments

Thank you is due to the Olive Baptist Church family. It is among them that I have proclaimed and tested the Eight Callings of God. These precious Christians have been my encouragers and prayer partners. Thank you for allowing me to be your pastor for these 19 plus years.

For many months three special ladies helped and encouraged me in this literary endeavor. Ginger Leonard served as my hermeneutical secretary and spent many hours putting this work together. My executive assistant, Beth Harris, has gone the extra mile chasing details to get this volume to the printer. And Carole Dunn gave hours reading the text and helping format the material. To these three I am extremely grateful.

No one encourages me more than my dear wife, Liz. Without her none of this would be possible. You are the best!

Table of Contents

Introduction

Are you glued to your cell phone? Attentive to your answering machine? Responsive to the telephone's ring? Are you anxious to know who called, why, if there's good news, interesting information, pleasure in the call and caller? Do you hope it's THE CALL you've been waiting for?

Responding to some calls produces negative results—bad news, inconvenience, annoyance, even anger. Some calls are disturbing, dangerous, or disgusting. Other calls can be wonderful, heartwarming, exciting, informative, and helpful. Such possibilities cause you to answer that ring or vibration, play back the messages, or return those calls. These are the motivators that make us choose to endure all those other calls.

Recorded messages offer some choice in responding. Obligation to job or family may require a response. Curiosity about the call and caller may generate an interested response. Knowing the caller and hoping for its content may produce an immediate and eager response. You can choose to avoid, ignore, forget, neglect, or delete calls. You can endure, resent, oblige, or refuse calls. All of these are choices. No doubt about it, our world is bombarded with busy, buzzing waves of communication.

God also calls. Are you listening, receiving His communication, comprehending His messages? Peter listed eight of His calls to Christians in 2 Peter 1:5-8. Have you received them, understood them, or replied to them?

These calls also present you with choices. God is calling believers to share in the divine nature, grow in His goodness, and escape the corruption surrounding us in this world. The cacophony of calls luring us to destruction can become the surround sounds of our lives, drowning out God's callings to the only truly good life.

From His initial call to salvation, through calls to moral excellence, knowledge, self-control, perseverance, godliness, and brotherly kindness to the final apex of love, God offers the power of preservation against the decay to mind, heart, body, and soul that this world imposes. According to 2 Peter 1:3-4, responding to these calls will give you a share in His divine nature. His perpetual power engenders a radical change and makes available to you everything you need for life and godliness. The choice to answer these callings is yours.

The following chapters seek to explain God's callings and to encourage you to respond to them. Hopefully, this study will lead you to escape corrupt influences and opt for that "good life." This is your greatest choice for all eternity.

1
The Calling of *Salvation*

"Joy to the world! the Lord is come." The melody to one of our most cherished songs was created with only one musical octave. George Frideric Handel used just eight tones to compose the well-known tune that he applied to that vibrant text from Psalm 98,

O SING TO THE LORD A NEW SONG...THE LORD HAS MADE KNOWN HIS SALVATION.

Second Peter 1:5-7 contains eight callings that can be likened to the eight notes found in a musical octave. The great preacher, Dr. W. A. Criswell, compared these callings to eight strands of thread put together to form a rope and interwoven to create strength. These eight biblical standards applied in our lives must be woven together before the beautiful song of faith can be completed on our soul's eternal score.

Peter says we are to build the octave of callings in our lives in the following progression:

To our **FAITH** , add
MORAL EXCELLENCE, to our moral excellence
KNOWLEDGE, to our knowledge
SELF-CONTROL, to our self-control
PERSEVERANCE, to our perseverance
GODLINESS, to our godliness
BROTHERLY KINDNESS, and to our brotherly kindness
LOVE.

Faith, our beginning keynote, is the calling of salvation. In John 6:35-40, Jesus defines this initial first calling of God to your life and mine.

> Jesus said to them, "I am the bread of life; he who comes to Me shall not hunger, and he who believes in Me shall never thirst. But I said to you that you have seen Me and yet do not believe. All that the Father gives Me shall come to Me, and the one who comes to Me I will certainly not cast out. For I have come down from heaven, not to do My own will, but the will of Him who sent Me. And this is the will of Him who sent Me, that of all that He has given Me I lose nothing, but raise it up on the last day. For this is the will of My Father, that everyone who beholds the Son and believes in Him, may have eternal life; and I Myself will raise him up on the last day."

FAITH CALLS US TO SALVATION

The first calling in your life must be to God's salvation. Unless you are saved you will never understand the other seven callings.

THE STAGES OF SALVATION

The stages of salvation include a past, a present and a future. In the book of Romans, Paul explains that he *was saved* in the past, he *was being saved* in the present, and he *will be saved* in the future. He *was saved* on the road to Damascus. He *was being saved* as he was being made more like Christ every day. And finally, he *will be saved* when he died and went to heaven. Our lives as believers must include a point we can look back to as the time when we *were saved.* Then, with Paul, we can say we *are being saved* as God works in us. Lastly, we *will be saved* when we die and go to heaven, our eternal home.

Every person needs salvation, for no one is righteous—no one. Every man, every woman, every boy, and every girl is a sinner. We were all born once, but we all must be born again. You will never come to faith in Christ until you admit, "I am lost. I am not right with God." Before you can be converted, you must understand that you are condemned, and that occurs through the convicting power of the Holy Spirit. It doesn't matter what you have done, how good you think you have been, or how much money you have given away. Until you understand you are lost, you will never come to faith in Christ. When you truly receive a revelation of the holiness of God, the Holy Spirit will convict you of the sinfulness of your own soul. Then you can accept God's free gift of grace, mercy, and salvation.

SALVATION INCLUDES A PAST, A PRESENT, AND A FUTURE

THE PICTURE OF SALVATION

Baptism and the Lord's Supper represent the picture of salvation. Both ordinances are to be a part of the believer's life.

Baptism publicly declares your profession of faith. First, there must be that experience in your life when the Spirit of God calls and you place your trust in Christ. This salvation is once and for all. After you are saved, then you should be baptized. This baptism is also a one-time experience. It testifies to others that Jesus Christ is your Savior. You have died to your old way of life and the "new you" is born.

The Lord's Supper (also called the Lord's Table, Communion, or the Eucharist) is the second picture of salvation in the church. The Lord's Supper is received not once, but on a continual basis. Each time you take the piece of bread and eat it, you are remembering the broken body of our Lord. You take the cup and drink in remembrance of Christ's blood shed for you. The renewal of your faith after baptism is ongoing throughout your life in Christ. Your worship through the ordinance of the Lord's Supper reflects your gratitude for this new life in Christ by His death on the cross.

THE ELEMENTS OF SALVATION

The elements of salvation are the plan, the assurance, and the evidence. All are found in the sixth chapter of the Gospel of John.

God has a plan of salvation

This plan, this calling of salvation, is found in John 6:37. Jesus says,

> All that the Father gives Me shall come to Me, and the one who comes to Me I will certainly not cast out.

The call to salvation seems to have two conflicting sides. The English word *come* used in verse 37 is translated from two different words in the Greek New Testament.

Jesus says that everyone the Father gives to Him will *come* to Him. Here the Greek word *heko* means they will definitely come. They have no choice in the matter. All the

Father chooses will come. God's Spirit calls, and God will draw them and bring them to Himself.

However, as Jesus continues, He says,

> And the one who comes to Me I will certainly not cast out.

The Greek word *erchomai* is used this time. In this instance, the word speaks of the decision one must make to come. Jesus delineates that some will definitely come and some will choose to come. As God calls, we choose to respond. Matthew 22:14 reads, "For many are called, but few are chosen." Galatians 1:6 teaches that we are called "by the grace of Christ." In 1 Corinthians 1:9 Paul writes, "God is faithful, through whom you were called into fellowship with His Son, Jesus Christ our Lord." In 1 Peter 5:10 he states, "…the God of all grace, who called you to His eternal glory in Christ, will Himself perfect, confirm, strengthen and establish you."

AS GOD CALLS, WE CHOOSE TO RESPOND

The age-old question is posed, "Is it the sovereignty of God or the free will of man that brings us to salvation?" This controversy has brewed through the ages. John 6:37*a* seems to say it is the sovereign call of God. Verse 37*b* seems to say it is the free will of man. Throughout the Reformation this debate continued. John Calvin, born in 1509, championed the view that the elective graces of God removed the choice for man.

He quoted John 6:44.

> No one can come to Me, unless the Father who sent Me draws him; and I will raise him up on the last day.

Arminius, a Dutch theologian born in 1560, was a proponent of free will. He believed that every man comes to Jesus when he gets ready. He has freedom, freedom, freedom! But consider this: if you are free to choose to be saved, then are you also free to become unsaved? Baptists say, "No!"

Examine the tension that exists. Which is it? Sovereignty or freedom? When I was saved, I made a choice. When God called me to salvation, I was ten years old, sitting in the church, seventh row from the back, attending Vacation Bible School. The day before, my pastor, Nolan Ford, inquired, "Ted, you've never been saved?"

I replied, "No, sir, I've never been saved."

The next day I was the first of sixteen children to walk down the aisle at the invitation time. I said, "Brother Nolan, you said Jesus died for me. I want to be saved." I knelt down and prayed, "Lord, come into my heart. Lord Jesus, save me." I was saved that very moment.

I believe if I had understood that day what I have come to understand today, I would have known that I was saved before the foundation of the world. My name was already written in the Lamb's Book of Life. I was an Arminian when I knelt down and a Calvinist when I stood up. Both exist in the sovereignty of God and the free will of man. But understand that to get out of balance on either side of this issue is to err biblically.

If you are an Arminian who believes it is all up to man, you will miss the sovereignty of God and the security of the believer. You will miss God's work in salvation. On the other hand, if you are in the sovereign camp—the Calvinistic side rather than the Arminian side—you might overreact and cease sharing the gospel. You may do away with missions altogether because, as some detractors told our early missionaries, if God wants to save somebody, He can do it without their help. Others propose we should stand in the middle of these two issues: sovereignty on one side, free will on the other. That attempt leads to madness! I believe, as one preacher stated, "You must go to both ends of this pole and go to the extreme in both issues."

You may say, "That doesn't make sense."

It doesn't make sense that the same water that contracts as it cools also expands as it freezes. It doesn't make sense that light consists of both waves and particles. The sovereignty of God alongside the free will of man doesn't make sense to many people either.

JESUS IS THE ONLY WAY

However, when you read the Bible, you will find both of them—much of the time on the same page. God's plan is salvation by the death and resurrection of His Son Jesus Christ, and there is no other way to heaven than through Jesus Christ our Lord. Jesus is the way and He will draw all men to Himself.

The Bible says in Isaiah 55:11,

> So shall My word be which goes forth from My mouth; it shall not return to Me empty, without accomplishing what I desire, and without succeeding in the matter for which I sent it.

When you preach the Word of God, you send it out. It will not return void. As you preach, God reaches out to accomplish His purposes.

Returning from a trip with my wife, Liz, we stopped at an outlet shopping mall in a neighboring town. A man I did not know called to me, "Pastor!"

Jokingly I answered, "I'm on vacation and off duty."

We shared a laugh and he continued, "Pastor, I listen to you every Sunday on the radio. God has a way of blessing my heart when you preach the message."

He further shared what God had been doing in his life through the witness of the preached Word of God. I didn't know he was out there listening and I hadn't contacted him personally, but through the sovereignty of God, His Word goes out and does its work according to God's purpose.

At the same time there are people such as a couple I visited not long ago. I aggravated them immensely by knocking on their door and calling their home over and over. Finally, they came to church, soon put their faith in Christ, and linked their lives with our church family. On one side sovereignty is at work. On the other side is the influence of man and the choices we make.

You may say, "I don't understand it."

Well, join the Baptist camp! I don't understand it either. As a matter of fact, I don't have to understand it.

You may ask, "Then is the Bible foolishness?"

No, the Bible is *mystery.* Just because these two sides of salvation seem contradictory does not make either less true. It is a mystery. God has chosen us before the foundation of the world, and He has called us to come to Him. Acts 2:21 states, "Everyone who calls on the name of the Lord shall be saved."

This is *His* plan of salvation.

God gives assurance of salvation

Not only does God have the plan of salvation, but secondly, He gives the assurance of salvation. Jesus states in John 6:39,

> And this is the will of Him who sent Me, that of all that He has given Me I lose nothing, but raise it up on the last day.

Do you understand that once you are saved you are always saved? Do you comprehend that when you come to Christ you are secure in Christ? Some people believe they can be saved today and lose their salvation tomorrow.

I have been told, "Preacher, I walked with God and was saved for fifteen years. Then I turned away from God and now I'm going to hell when I die." That person has not understood the Word of God. Jesus said if you are His, He will never lose you. The Bible says Jesus is in God's hand; you are in Jesus' hand, and no man can pluck you out (John 10:29). You and I may have lost things before, but Jesus doesn't lose things and He's not going to lose you.

YOUR SALVATION IS SECURE

When a surveyor determines the boundary of a piece of property, he drives down a stake to mark a definite location. In our salvation experience, there are some stakes we need to drive down that will bring assurance of our salvation. What are these stakes?

Confession of Jesus as Lord

If you have doubts about your salvation, it might be because you have sin in your life that you have not forsaken. If you are not growing in your faith, 2 Peter 1 says you will doubt your purification. If you come to the place where you do not believe the Word of God, you will most likely doubt your salvation. Confession is the first stake to drive down in your Christian life. Romans 10:9-10 explains,

> That if you confess with your mouth Jesus as Lord, and believe in your heart that God raised Him from the dead, you shall be saved; for with the heart man believes, resulting in righteousness, and with the mouth he confesses, resulting in salvation.

Confirmation of the Holy Spirit

Confirmation of the Holy Spirit is the next stake. Romans 8:16 says,

> The Spirit Himself bears witness with our spirit that we are children of God.

When you confess with your mouth, the Spirit of God begins to confirm with your spirit that you are a child of God. Thus, another stake is driven down validating your salvation.

I heard a story about a boy who began doubting his salvation. The preacher told him that Romans 10:13 says,

> ...Whoever will call upon the name of the Lord will be saved.

The boy took a two-by-four and wrote Romans 10:13 on the board. Then he took a hammer, went out behind the barn, and drove his stake down deep into the ground. The next time the boy doubted he was really saved, he went out to the barn, pulled up his stake and looked at what he had written.

> ...Whoever will call upon the name of the Lord will be saved.

He held the board in the direction where he thought the devil would be and shouted, "Listen to me, devil. This is the promise of God, and I'm staking my life on it." Satisfied, he drove it back down into the ground and walked away with assurance.

Confession through baptism

Finally, you need to drive down the stake of confession through baptism. God brings assurance in your heart through the ordinance of baptism. Baptism by immersion is the outward public confession of what has transpired privately in your life. You are publicly declaring through this symbol that you have died to your old self and have been raised to walk in your new life as a believer. Baptism is a one-time assertion declaring that Jesus is your Lord.

There must be a confession with your mouth, a confirmation of the Holy Spirit, and confession through baptism. These three declarations bring confidence and reassurance in the truth of salvation. As doubts creep in throughout your life (and they will), grab hold of these stakes and hammer them down again, and again, and again. Stake the very assurance of your eternal life on them, and hold fast to your salvation.

God gives evidence of salvation

We have examined the plan of salvation, the assurance of salvation, and now we inspect the evidence of salvation. John 6:40 says,

> For this is the will of My Father, that everyone who beholds the Son and believes in Him, may have eternal life; and I Myself will raise him up on the last day.

When you have eternal life, there will be *evidence* of that life. I have physical life, and there is evidence of that physical life. I've had evidence of that for more than fifty years. Some of you have lived seventy years. The evidence of that is your hair is falling out. At the end of the day some of you are going to take your teeth out—evidence you've been here eighty years. Some of you couldn't climb stairs if you wanted to—evidence you've been here ninety years. But you have life, and there's evidence of that life. You're still breathing. You're still eating. You're still going. Some of you are still complaining. Some of you are still rejoicing. Some of you are still smiling. You see, there is evidence when there is life. Eternal life produces six evidences:

CHANGES IN YOU ARE PROOF OF YOUR ETERNAL LIFE

- **A new awareness of right and wrong**
- **A hunger for the Word of God**
- **A desire for a changed life**
- **An increase in testing**
- **A love for other Christians**
- **A desire to tell others about Jesus**

These six evidences are proof of eternal life. The first evidence is a *new awareness of right and wrong*. John 16:8 says of the Holy Spirit,

> And He, when He comes, will convict the world concerning sin, and righteousness, and judgment.

When you are saved, you have a new understanding of what is right and what is wrong. The Spirit of God living in you will reprove you of sin in your life, of the righteousness that should be in your life, and of the judgment that will come from God.

While I was a student in college, I attended a Civitan meeting in Orlando, Florida. After the last session, I found myself in a bar with my friends. Suddenly I heard the Spirit of God say to me, "You do not belong in this place." He was reproving me of sin, of a righteous stand, and a judgment to come. When the Spirit of God moves in and takes up residence within us, He brings a new awareness of right and wrong.

Second, you will have a *hunger for the Word of God.* Hebrews 5:14 says,

> But solid food is for the mature, who because of practice have their senses trained to discern good and evil.

When you are saved, you have a new appetite. If you can go ten, fifteen, or twenty years and never have a desire to read the Word of God, you should have some doubt about your reservation in heaven. If you can go months and months and never have concern for the Word of God, I do not know if you have ever experienced the Bread of Life. If you ever taste the sweetness of Scripture, you will understand that it is, as the psalmist described, like honey to your soul. It brings strength to you that nothing else gives. The evidence of eternal life is a hunger for the Word of God.

The third evidence is a *desire for a changed life.* Second Corinthians 5:17 says,

> Therefore if any man is in Christ, he is a new creature; the old things passed away; behold, new things have come.

When you come to faith in Christ, you want a changed life. You desire things to be different. The past is your old creature, and when you are saved, you want to be new. You want to start over and live a life pleasing to your Lord. It doesn't mean you will do right every time or be perfect. It does mean you have a desire for a changed life.

The fourth evidence is an *increase in testing.* Second Timothy 3:12 says,

> And indeed, all who desire to live godly in Christ Jesus will be persecuted.

When you begin to take a stand for Christ in this world, persecution will come in your life. If nothing is bothering you, you may not be bothering the devil. When you live for God, the wicked one becomes riled and launches his attack against you. James 1:2 gives us a reminder.

> Consider it all joy, my brethren, when you encounter various trials.

When testing comes in abundance, count it as evidence of eternal life.

The fifth evidence of salvation is a *love for other Christians*. First John 4:7 says,

> Beloved, let us love one another, for love is from God; and everyone who loves is born of God and knows God.

Recently I had somebody ask me about a certain individual, "Do you love him?"

I replied, "Oh yeah, I love him. I just don't trust him."

John did not say you have to trust everybody. If somebody, as we say, stabs you in the back several times, you may not be able to trust him completely, but you do have to love him. Jesus instructed us to love others as much as we love ourselves (Matthew 22:39). First Corinthians 13 describes that kind of love. Love is kind, but love also speaks the truth. Tough love can still be Christian love. Love for fellow believers is evidence of salvation.

Finally, the sixth evidence of eternal life is a *desire to tell others about Jesus Christ*. Psalm 107:2 says,

> Let the redeemed of the Lord say so.

When you know Christ and know you are going to heaven, you want to tell somebody. You want to share the gospel with others. If you are the redeemed of the Lord, you want to speak up and say so!

> THE FIRST NOTE
> IS
> FAITH

The plan of salvation is this: you were born a sinner, Christ died for you, and He wants to forgive you, come into your heart and save you. When He does, He wants to become your best friend all the way to the end of life.

He will receive you if you confess your sin—your need—and His adequacy. *Faith* is the first calling of God through His salvation. Will you respond to that calling and say "Yes, Lord, yes"?

REPEAT

1. List the eight callings of God found in 2 Peter 1:5-7.

   ____

   ____

   ____

   ____

   ____

   ____

   ____

   ____

2. Faith is the calling to ______________________.

3. What are the three elements of salvation found in John 6?

   ____

   ____

   ____

4. List the stakes you can drive down in your life to counteract doubts that may arise regarding your salvation.

5. What are the six evidences of your eternal life?

INTERPRET

6. Can you identify the time and place, the when and where you were when you confessed Jesus as your Lord and received salvation? List those facts below.

7. Why is faith the keynote of these eight callings?

8. How would you describe the sovereignty of God in your salvation?

9. How would you explain the part your free will had in your salvation?

PRACTICE

10. If you have not confessed your need and confessed that Jesus is Lord to receive His salvation, will you do that now?

11. If you have accepted His salvation but experience doubts, which stakes of assurance are wobbly? What are you going to do to hammer them down securely?

PAUSE

Father, I thank You for Your plan and assurance of my salvation that makes me Your child. Let me be nourished at Your table on the Bread of Life–Your Word. Let me taste the sweetness of its truth and teachings. Increase my desire to tell others the good news of Your salvation. May I throughout all the days of my life say "Yes, Lord, yes." In the name of Jesus, I pray. Amen.

2
The Calling of *Separation*

The next note in our octave is the second calling of God, the call to separation. Peter makes clear that beginning with your

FAITH you are to add
MORAL EXCELLENCE, to your moral excellence add
KNOWLEDGE, to your knowledge add
SELF-CONTROL, to your self-control add
PERSEVERANCE, to your perseverance add
GODLINESS, to your godliness add
BROTHERLY KINDNESS, and to your brotherly kindness add
LOVE.

Understand this: Christian maturity does not come instantaneously. It is a process constantly moving us toward acquiring these qualities. Peter instructs that if these traits are ours and are increasing in our lives, we can obtain great assurance that we are children of God.

The calling of salvation begins with faith. And now to our faith we add moral excellence. Moral excellence is the calling of separation.

In 2 Corinthians 6:14-7:1, Paul writes,

> Do not be bound together with unbelievers; for what partnership have righteousness and lawlessness, or what fellowship has light with darkness? Or what harmony has Christ with Belial, or what has a believer in common with an unbeliever? Or what agreement has the temple of God with idols? For we are the temple of the living God; just as God said, "I will dwell in them and walk among them; and I will be their God, and they shall be My people. Therefore, come out from their midst and be separate," says the Lord. "And do not touch what is unclean; and I will welcome you. And I will be a father to you, and you shall be sons and daughters to Me," says the Lord Almighty. Therefore, having these promises, beloved, let us cleanse ourselves from all defilement of flesh and spirit, perfecting holiness in the fear of God.

The first lesson a Christian must learn and the first discipline we must master is to be separate from the world, for either we separate ourselves from all forms of evil, or evil will separate us from our fellowship with God. You cannot be separated back into a lost condition. However, unless you master the discipline of being separate from the world, this world's spirit will cost you intimate companionship with God. Isaiah 59:2 says to us,

> But your iniquities have made a separation between you and your God, and your sins have hidden His face from you, so that He does not hear.

Psalm 66:18 gives a warning.

> If I regard wickedness in my heart, the Lord will not hear.

The iniquity we hold on to will draw a curtain between God and us, and He will not hear us. We must be separate from the world, but also be separated *unto Christ.* When you separate yourself from the spirit of the world and receive the spirit of Christ—when you separate yourself unto Him—you will experience Christ-originated joy and be full of the glory of God.

BE SEPARATED UNTO CHRIST

There are three distinctions related to the calling of separation. First is the principle of separation. Second is the power of separation. And third is the promise of separated living.

THE PRINCIPLE OF SEPARATION

In 2 Corinthians 6:14, Paul declares, "Do not be bound together with unbelievers."

This is the first principle: the principle of separation. The phrase *bound together with unbelievers* is derived from the Greek word *heterozugeo.* Dividing the word leads to the discovery of its meaning. The first part, *heteros*, denotes "other" or "different." The second part, *zugos*, is the word for "yoke." When the words are combined, Paul's meaning is clear: believers are not to be yoked together with people who are different from them. That is exactly what is described in Deuteronomy 22:10.

> You shall not plow with an ox and a donkey together.

Why not? Because the step and the strength of an ox and a donkey are not alike. The step and the strength of a believer and an unbeliever are different. We are to be yoked only with fellow believers.

During a visit to the home of one of my church deacons, I saw a clear (and humorous) illustration of this principle. On my fortieth birthday—which happened to fall on a Sunday—the church choir surprised me by singing "Happy Birthday" while holding up 8x10 photos of my face. The deacon took one of those pictures, framed it, and put it on the wall at his home. Hanging next to my picture was a picture of a popular president whose lifestyle differed greatly from mine. I told him, "That, my friend, is being unequally yoked together." We laughed, but much later when I visited again in his home, the president's picture had been removed and my picture remained!

As a believer, there are some people with whom you do not associate and there are some places and positions where you do not belong. You will be *heterozugeo*—unequally yoked together. Moreover, God says when you are saved, you are to, "Come out from among them and be ye separate" (2 Corinthians 6:17).

How do we apply this principle to our daily lives? First, let's consider what it does *not* mean. It does not mean you are to have no friends in the world of unbelievers. Paul explains in 1 Corinthians 5:9-13.

> I wrote you in my letter not to associate with immoral people; I did not at all mean with the immoral people of this world, or with the covetous and swindlers, or with idolaters; for then you would have to go out of the world. But actually, I wrote to you not to associate with any so-called brother if he should be an

> immoral person, or covetous, or an idolater, or a reviler, or a drunkard, or a swindler—not even to eat with such a one. For what have I to do with judging outsiders? Do you not judge those who are within the church? But those that are outside, God judges. Remove the wicked man from among yourselves.

When Paul instructs us to come out and be separate, he is not stating that we should have no acquaintances in the lost world. We must. You would have to leave this world entirely to avoid all association with unbelieving people. But our presence in this world requires us to be like salt and light. We must not allow the spirit of the unbelieving world to become our spirit.

Another important area where the principle of separation does *not* relate is in our marriage commitment. If you become saved and your spouse remains lost, you are not to divorce your unsaved spouse. I have had married people come to me after being saved—their spouse still unsaved—and announce that God was leading them to divorce the lost mate and "go out and be separate."

No! The Word of God does not teach that mistaken belief. That is not the teaching of separation. Paul specifically speaks to this situation in 1 Corinthians 7:12-16.

> But to the rest I say, not the Lord, [Paul is not implying that what he is about to write is not scripture; he is simply saying that Jesus has not spoken to this, but he, Paul, is still under inspiration] that if any brother has a wife who is an unbeliever, and she consents to live with him, let him not send her away. And a woman who has an unbelieving husband, and he

> consents to live with her, let her not send her husband away. For the unbelieving husband is sanctified through his wife, and the unbelieving wife is sanctified through the believing husband; for otherwise your children are unclean, but now they are holy. Yet if the unbelieving one leaves, let him leave; the brother or the sister is not under bondage in such cases, but God has called us to peace. For how do you know, O wife, whether you will save your husband? Or how do you know, O husband, whether you will save your wife?

When two unbelievers are married and one comes to faith in Christ, this calling of separation does not imply that the saved spouse is allowed to divorce the unsaved spouse. Regrettably, that is a false teaching that has infiltrated the local church.

The spirit of the world poisons our lives and paralyzes our testimony

So, what does this principle of separation stand for? In 1 Corinthians 2:12 Paul says,

> Now we have received, not the spirit of the world, but the Spirit who is from God.

THE BELIEVER NOW HAS THE SPIRIT OF GOD

When we come to faith in Christ, we are still living in the world, but now we have the Spirit of God within us. We are not to participate with the spirit of this world any longer. James 4:4 warns that friendship with the world is enmity with God. Beware: the spirit of this lost world is like an insidious toxin. It will invade your Christianity, poison your life, and paralyze your testimony.

The spirit of the world is insensitive to and passive toward Christ

The spirit of this world will try to accomplish two things against you. First, it will cause you to be insensitive in spiritual matters. It will annihilate your discernment. You will become insensitive toward people who are hurting and become a legalist in your faith.

Second, the spirit of this world will cause you to become passive in scriptural matters. The spirit of this world says, "I know what the Bible says, but…" or "I know what Scripture teaches, but…." It will cause you to yield truth in scriptural matters to the untruth of the world opinions. Passiveness yields to compromise. Be very careful not to become coupled with the spirit of this world.

Notice what Paul says in 2 Corinthians 6:14-16. He uses five descriptive associations between the believer (the one in the light) and unbeliever (the one who is in the darkness). He asks,

"what partnership…
what fellowship…
what harmony…
what in common… or
what agreement…"
…can there be between believers and unbelievers?

Each time the answer is absolutely none. We have no partnership. We have no harmony. We have no fellowship. We have nothing in common. We have no agreement with the spirit of this world.

Legalism would decree numerous laws and demands on the believer such as, "If you're going to be a Christian, then you must never go to that kind of movie or to this type of activity." But legalism must yield to discernment. We must discern what will bring us closer to the Spirit of Christ and discern what will help us stay away from all things that pull us toward the spirit of the world.

When you move toward loving Jesus with all your heart, you will confront the issue of separation. That confrontation is exactly why some people have never been saved. They attend church, hear a preacher proclaim the cross and the resurrection, and still they say, "I'd come give my heart and life to God, but I'm not willing to give up A-B-C. I'm not willing to stop doing X-Y-Z." Actually, these people are not ready to be S-A-V-E-D. A person must be willing to come to Christ on His terms alone, and those terms include separation.

A common response is, "I don't have the power to do all that." No one does. God gives us His power. What we must have is an enthusiastic spirit to proclaim, "I'm ready to say *no* to the world and *yes* to Christ."

The spirit of the world must be avoided

How do we avoid intimacy with an unbelieving world in this calling of separation? We must give attention to three vital areas of our lives.

Avoid the practices of the unbelieving world

First, we need to avoid intimacy with unbelieving practices. The spirit of this world tells us some ways are right, but we believers should have no tolerance for the ways of the world.

CHRISTIANS MUST NOT SUPPORT EVIL PRACTICES

An example of one of these practices is abortion. Abortion is a sin before God. It is a heinous crime. America turned its back on the Creator when the legal system ruled that abortion is legal and right, but it will never be right. God will never sanction it. He is never pleased with abortion.

There are scores of women (including members of churches) who have been convinced by the spirit of this world to choose abortion as a legitimate way to end their pregnancies. The spirit of the world says, "Abort the fetus. It's okay. It's not a person until it is born." Scripture declares the opposite. God told Jeremiah, "Before I formed you in the womb I knew you, and before you were born I consecrated you" (Jeremiah 1:5). Abortion on demand is always wrong, and believers must stop entering abortion clinics. Intimacy with the spirit of this world will lead to corrupt practices, so we must learn to avoid them and walk in our calling of separation.

Come out and be ye separate, says the Lord.

Avoid going to the wrong places in the unbelieving world

Just as there are some practices we should not participate in, there are some places we should not go. If God has called you out to be separate, then He will help you recognize the places where you may go and the places you should *never* go. There are wicked establishments in every

CHRISTIANS DON'T BELONG IN SOME PLACES

city where godless activities take place in the name of entertainment. How sad that even church members can be found in these places. Just because it is legal doesn't make it right for the believer. If a person feels he has to sneak in to avoid being seen, chances are it is a place he shouldn't be in at all. And if we could get all the Christians to stop going to these places, many of them would have to close down. (You know I'm telling the truth.) There are some places we as believers don't belong.

Come out and be ye separate, says the Lord.

Avoid fellowship with some people in the unbelieving world

Finally, we do not belong with some people. Be cautious in your business partnerships. Beware of yoking yourself with unbelievers in financial relationships. The spirit of the world will always cause conflict with the ways of God. Be careful in choosing your intimate friends. Remember Paul's warning. Believers and unbelievers have little harmony with one another.

If there is any place where we are ultimately yoked, it is with a spouse, and God will not lead you to marry an unbeliever. Deciding whether or not to marry a person should not be determined by the answer to the question, "Is this person a Christian?" The most important question should be, "Is this person a *growing* Christian?" If you want to have true partnership and fellowship, marry someone who is moving toward God in his or her daily walk.

MARRIAGE IS NOT AN EVANGELISTIC TOOL

Occasionally I am reprimanded by women who say, "But, Pastor, I married an unbeliever and I won him to the Lord." Unfortunately this is far from the norm in most relationships. Marriage is not an evangelistic tool in the New Testament.

There are some people in the unbelieving world who it is wiser to avoid.

Come out and be ye separate, says the Lord.

Our calling is to separation. The calling is to come out from certain *practices*, certain *places*, and certain *people*.

THE POWER OF SEPARATION

After learning the principle of separation, the believer should consider the power of separation. When a Christian learns to be separate, God's power will dominate his life. There are scores of church members who never enter the doors of the church and by all accounts do not live their lives for Jesus. But if they would separate themselves toward God and away from the spirit of the world, we would see true revival. The power of God will come upon a separated heart.

God says in 2 Corinthians 6:16-17,

> I will dwell in them and walk among them; and I will be their God, and they shall be My people. Therefore, come out from their midst and be separate.

God will work for you, He will work in you, and He will work through you. He will show Himself strong on your behalf if you will come out and be separated from the spirit of this world.

More than any other character in the Old Testament, the story of Samson teaches us about the power found in separation. In the book of Judges, chapters 13-16, we are introduced to Samson. He was a man's man. Samson would have been part of the World Wrestling Federation. He would have been drafted as a linebacker or tight end by the NFL. Samson was the strongest man who ever lived.

Before he was born, his parents dedicated him to be a Nazirite all his life. A Nazirite was someone bound by a vow to be set apart for the service of God. A Nazirite could not do three things. A Nazirite had to leave his hair uncut. A Nazirite could not partake of the fruit of the vine. And a Nazirite had to remain free from all impurities, including touching dead bodies. As long as Samson walked in these vows the power of God rested on his life.

However, in his adult life, Samson violated all three of these vows. He went to a party—a seven day feast—where there was undoubtedly a lot of wine flowing, and we can be fairly certain he broke the vow not to drink alcohol. (He had no qualms breaking the rest of his vows.) He scooped out honey from the carcass of a lion, and by touching the dead body, broke that vow of a Nazirite. Then he wound up in Delilah's barbershop and she cut his hair. Again, he broke the Nazirite vow. The Bible says the Philistines came and bound Samson, gouged out his eyes, and made a foolish display of him. Samson had entered into the spirit of the world.

However, Judges 16 tells us that Samson's hair began to grow back. When he was brought to the temple of the Philistines' pagan god, he put his hands on the two middle pillars that supported the old temple and pleaded with God in Judges 16:28.

> O Lord God, please remember me and please strengthen me just this time. . . .

In that moment Samson renewed his separation unto God. He cried out,

> Let me die with the Philistines!

The Bible says he pushed those pillars with all his might and the temple collapsed. Over three thousand Philistines were killed and their temple was destroyed. The power of God came back upon Samson's life, but what a waste!

Like Samson, some of us waste our strength on the spirit of the world. If we would ever commit to being separated unto Jesus, unto loving Him with all our hearts, the power of God would come upon us and He could use us a thousand-fold. It is not a simply a matter of being separated from the world. We must be separated unto God.

Alan Redpath wrote that separation entails investing each moment of every day in commitment to God's authority in our lives and allowing His power to rule without reservation and to the glory of God. This means living so as not to disturb or disrupt your harmony with holy God—the harmony between you and the Father. When you are separated unto Him, His power will rest upon you.

KEEP AN UNDISTURBED HARMONY WITH GOD

THE PROMISE OF SEPARATION

Not only do we see the principle and the power, but thirdly there is the promise of separation found in Second Corinthians 6:18. If you will separate yourself to Jesus and Jesus alone, God gives His word.

> And I will be a Father to you, and you shall be sons and daughters to Me.

Here is the promise: if you will live for God, He will be your Father. Do you have a father who loves you?

In December 2004, my daughter, Rachel, was in two accidents that totaled two vehicles in twenty-two hours. (A new record with our insurance company!) The first was on a Monday afternoon. She stopped at a red light and the sixteen-year-old driving behind her did not. He rear-ended her car, slamming her into the truck in front of her. The car was a total loss. The policeman was amazed Rachel walked away with only bruising from her seat belt.

The next day she went to the doctor to have her shoulder checked, and then to the dentist. As she left the office a speeding car slammed into her again, this time totaling her mother's vehicle. My daughter was shaken up, but fine, just very sore. When that first accident happened, we walked through it pretty well. With the second accident, it wasn't quite the same.

When the phone call came that day, I was at home. I answered the phone.

"Hello?"

All I heard was "Daddy!" and then squalling.

"Rachel?"

A woman came on the phone and asked, "Sir, are you Mr. Traylor?"

"I am."

She said, "Your daughter's had a wreck."

"I know. She had a wreck yesterday afternoon."

The voice on the other end said, "Oh no, no. She had a wreck just moments ago."

I said, "Put my daughter back on the phone."

When I got her on the phone, she said, "Daddy!" and then there was some more squalling.

"Darlin', I'll be there as fast as I can."

If you are serious about being separated unto God, He will be a Father to you. And we've all had those times, haven't we? Something happens and we begin crying out to the

Father. But the Bible says if you regard iniquity in your heart, God does not hear you. However, when you come clean with God and separate yourself to Him and cry out to Him, God will be a Father to you and you will be His son or daughter.

You see, our God is a jealous God. He loves you, but He will not tolerate "playing games" in your relationship with Him. If you don't get serious with God, observe what Paul cautions in 2 Corinthians 11:2-3.

> For I am jealous for you with a godly jealousy; for I betrothed you to one husband, that to Christ I might present you as a pure virgin.

Paul is saying that because the church is the bride of Christ, she has only one husband. There is only one Man for the church and His name is Jesus. Paul continues,

> But I am afraid, lest as the serpent deceived Eve by his craftiness, your minds should be led astray from the simplicity and purity of devotion to Christ.

What happens when that satanic deception comes upon you? You get caught up in the spirit of the world. You want to be popular. You want to be wealthy. You want this world to say, "Well done" rather than hear God say, "Well done!" You are deceived, and the craftiness of the devil draws you away from God.

Imagine this scenario. My wife, Liz, leaves town for a long weekend to take care of her mother. Imagine I contact our singles division and get three or four of the unmarried girls to come on over to our house. They clean and cook and take great care of me. They do the laundry and fold my clothes. I even have one of them wash my car. Imagine I have to fly to Atlanta early the next morning, so they have my bags packed and have breakfast ready for me. While I'm gone, they'll make sure everything is taken care of and the cat gets fed. When I get back, they will pick me up at the airport and bring me home. These single ladies are taking great care of me while Liz is away.

Now really! Do you think for one moment my wife would put up with that? Not for a minute! As she's said to me many times, "If I come home and you've messed up, we won't be talking reconciliation. We'll be talking resurrection!"

As my wife is zealously jealous of our marriage commitment, our God is a jealous God over His relationship with you. You may not have more than one Father just as you are not to have more than one spouse. You are supposed to have only one. We have lost the purity of our commitment to Christ. We have said we can be "married" to Jesus and live with the world at the same time. Remember, Paul said, "I have betrothed you unto one" (2 Corinthians 11:2).

If you have an earthly father who loves you, you understand the promise of separation unto the heavenly Father. After Rachel had her two accidents, do you know who *I* called? I called my daddy. I said, "Dad, before I tell you anything else, I want you to know your only granddaughter is okay. The apple of your eye is all right. I just want you to know she's fine. But your son, he ain't doin' too good." That day I needed to hear my father's voice. But even more than that, I need daily to hear the voice of my Father call me His son.

How do we determine what makes us separated unto God? How do you know if what you are involved in is right or wrong?

Ask yourself the following six questions about any activity:

- **Is what I'm doing for the glory of God?**
- **Does it have the appearance of evil?**
- **Is it a stumbling stone to weaker Christians?**
- **Will it be a weight that drags me down?**
- **Does it make my prayer life more difficult?**
- **Can I ask God's blessing on it?**

THERE ARE WAYS TO KNOW THE RIGHT THING TO DO

I'm from the country in Alabama, but I grew up in the grocery store business, so I didn't know much about rural life. But the farmers came into our store and I got to know them, and every now and then I'd get hired for a small job in the *real* country. I'll never forget the day I went out to work on a farm for a man who had two mules. He harnessed them up and said, "Would you like to plow?"

My spirit said *no* but my mouth said, "Sure." My pride said, *Why, yeah, anybody can do this.*

Those two mules were naturally alike in step and strength to one another, but I still couldn't keep them plowing in a straight line. I found out that not just anybody can plow. And I couldn't help thinking about the biblical illustration of the yoke. Suppose one of those mules was replaced by a different kind of animal? Then I would have had two unequally yoked animals. They would not have pulled together and the plowing would have been an even bigger mess.

What messes up our churches today? It's when Christians try to be yoked with Jesus and with the spirit of the world. When that happens we're plowing like my grandmother described as "every-which-a-way." As a matter of fact, that's not plowing at all. We're spending all our time trying to keep two things in harmony that can never agree.

MORAL EXCELLENCE THAT CALLS US TO SEPARATION IS OUR SECOND NOTE

The first call of God is this: come by faith to the Christ who died for you. He'll forgive you. He'll love you. He'll save you and change you. The second call is to separate yourself from the spirit of the world and be separate unto the Father.

Well, after hanging up the phone that day after the second wreck, I drove to the site of the accident. When I pulled up, I wasn't looking for a police officer. I wasn't looking for the person who hit my girl. I wasn't looking to see if the car could be fixed. I was looking for just one special person. And when my daughter saw me, she came running and I started running toward her. I held her in my arms as she cried on my shoulder.

I said, "Darlin', it'll be okay."

"Daddy, I thought you'd be mad."

"No, I'm not mad. Are you okay?"

She said, "Daddy, the car…"

"Don't worry about the car. There are all kinds of paint and metal in this world. We can find some more of that. Are you okay?"

"Yeah, Daddy, I'm fine—now that you're here."

When you are separated unto God, there will be times when you need to fall into your Father's arms. I have great news. You come running! He has His arms wide open welcoming whosever will, whosoever will come and be separate unto the Lord Jesus Christ.

REPEAT

1. List the eight callings of God found in 2 Peter 1:5-7.

____

____

____

____

____

____

____

____

2. Moral excellence is the call to ______________________________.

3. We are to be separated from ________________________ and unto ____.

4. What are three distinctions of this separation?

INTERPRET

5. Why is it important to be separated not only from the world but also unto Christ?

6. How can you identify the practices, places, and people from which you should be separated?

PRACTICE

7. What specific practices, places, and/or people need to be separated from your life?

8. How do you propose to accomplish this?

9. What steps do you intend to take toward separation unto Christ?

PAUSE

Father, thank You for the truth of Your Word. Thank You for revealing the need for separation from the world. And even more I ask that I be separated toward You. I ask to experience the power of separation in my life. Let me fall into Your arms as I am Your child and You are indeed my Father. All this I pray in Jesus' blessed name. Amen.

3
The Calling of
Sanctification

Like eight notes found in a musical octave from which beautiful melodies are composed, so God uses the eight callings given in 2 Peter 1:5-7 to bring the music of Himself into our lives. God desires to orchestrate these attributes into each of us and cause our lives to resonate with Him. Read again what this scripture says, that beginning with your

FAITH you are to add
MORAL EXCELLENCE, to your moral excellence add
KNOWLEDGE, to your knowledge add
SELF-CONTROL, to your self-control add
PERSEVERANCE, to your perseverance add
GODLINESS, to your godliness add
BROTHERLY KINDNESS, and to your brotherly kindness add
LOVE.

Like eight tones played together to form a melodious chord, so God scores our lives into His when we obey and apply these callings He has set for us to follow.

We began with *faith*, which is the calling of salvation. Next we added *moral excellence*, and that is the calling of separation. Now we add to our moral excellence *knowledge*. This is the calling of sanctification. First you are saved, and then you separate from that old sin life as the power of God comes into your life. As you move

TRUTH WILL MAKE YOU FREE

toward sanctification, you become a positive influence for God.

Knowledge that leads to sanctification comes from truth. Truth will make you free. In John 8:31-32, Jesus speaks about this sanctifying power that is ours through Him and through His Word.

> If you abide in My word [*if you live in the Word*] then you are truly disciples of Mine; [*one of the proofs, staying in the Word*] and you shall know the truth [*if you abide in the Word*] and the truth shall make you free.

Knowledge is a marvelous thing, but it can be used for good or bad. Knowledge can be used to create a super fiend, an oppressor, and a killer of thousands. Terrorists are shaped by untrue, counterfeit knowledge. They believe the wrong ideals and have zeal through false knowledge that leads to a twisted fanaticism. Or knowledge can be used to create a bondservant of the Lord Jesus Christ. Your life can be defined by the knowledge you have and the use and application of that knowledge.

In the Greek New Testament, when the letter *a* is placed before a word, it forms the negative, creating the opposite meaning. When you put the negative with the word *theos,* which means "God," you form the word *atheos* (without God). From this we derive the English word *atheist* (no God). Again, by placing the letter *a* at the beginning of the word *gnosis,* from which we get our word *knowledge*, we form *agnosis* or the English word *agnostic*. An atheist is one who does not believe in God. Agnostics are not atheists. Agnostics do not have enough knowledge to prove there is a God. They admit there might be a God, but there is not enough evidence to confirm to them that there is a God.

The atheist is the most self-righteous person in the world. An atheist says, “I know everything, therefore I know God does not exist.” But the agnostic says, “I don’t know everything. There may be a God. I just don’t know enough yet to be sure there is one.” Jesus replies to both of these views by proclaiming in His Word that if you come to know the truth, the truth will set you free.

I am told it would take 147 years to complete all the courses offered at Harvard University. That’s quite an education to pack into your head, and it is your head I am after now. In chapter one we considered the condition of your heart. And if God can capture your heart (faith) *and* your head (knowledge), He will do a fresh work within you. Jesus promises freedom and truth. These will produce sanctified living. I want to focus upon truth and the calling of sanctification. In John 8:31-32, there are three issues that address this calling in our lives. The first is *the source of truth*, then *the study of truth,* and finally the *strength of truth.*

LET GOD HAVE YOUR HEART AND HEAD

THE SOURCE OF TRUTH

Truth must be found. What is truth? Where is its source? The Muslim says he knows truth. The Hindu says he knows truth. As stated earlier, atheists and agnostics have their views concerning truth. On and on we could go listing “truth” in this world full of beliefs based on false “facts.”

Liz and I went out to eat recently and she picked up a newspaper published by the Universalist Church. This newspaper printed many ideas about truth—metaphysical phenomena, séances, all kinds of weird stuff. Spiritualists proclaimed that God is in us when we are born and each of us is God. Now, I’ve been a lot of things but I am not God. I’ll let you in on a little something—you are not God either. And our universalist friends will know this when they die—they are not God. God has come among us, and *Jesus is His name!*

There are three sources of truth. I call them the person of truth, the place of truth, and the page of truth.

The Person of Truth

Jesus says to "abide in My word" (John 8:31). There you will find truth. You will find the *person* of truth. Jesus says about Himself in John 14:6, "I am the way, the truth…." He is the truth. I am not the person of truth; you are not the person of truth. The person of truth is Jesus Christ.

The Place of Truth

The place of truth can be found in Scripture. The Bible says in 1 Timothy 3:15 that the church is the pillar and the ground of truth. That word "ground" means the church is the buttress or the fortress. The church is the place that holds up truth. Let me give you a warning here: if you find yourself in a church where the Bible is not believed and truth is not proclaimed, get out! Life is too short to live with a group of liberals who think they know more about God than God knows about Himself. Truth is always based on what God says, never on what we may think when it is contrary to God's Word.

The Page of Truth

There is the person of truth, the place of truth, and the page of truth, which is the Word of God. Second Timothy 2:15 teaches that the Bible is the Word of truth. Ninety-two percent of Americans own at least one Bible (three per household, on average) and that includes practicing Christians and hundreds of thousands of atheists. Even with all those Bibles, 58 percent of Americans cannot tell you who preached the Sermon on the Mount, 63 percent cannot name the four gospels (only 50 percent can name any), and only 42 percent can name at least five of the Ten Commandments.[1] We have in America a host of people who have been down the church aisle, knelt, prayed to receive salvation, and even been baptized. Sadly most have stopped right there in their Christian lives. They have never answered the call of separation to moral excellence or the call to knowledge of God's Word which leads to sanctified living.

TRUTH
IS BASED ON WHAT
GOD SAYS

Ephesians 5:25-26 is a well-known passage usually assigned as a marriage illustration, but here we see an important application to the call of knowledge.

> Husbands, love your wives, just as Christ also loved the church and gave Himself up for her that He might sanctify her…

There it is—the calling of sanctification. Jesus gave Himself up for the church. He died for the church so that He could sanctify the church. The word *sanctify* here is the Greek word *hagiazo.* It means holy, set apart, clean.

> … having cleansed her by the washing of water with the Word.

Do you know that Jesus washes His church? He washes it with the water of the Word. In the Old Testament, the Jewish tabernacle is a typology of Christ. Before entering into the Holy of Holies, the high priest would wash his hands in the laver, a large basin used by the ancient Jewish priests for ceremonial washing. This symbolized the cleansing of sin before a priest could enter the tabernacle door. In referencing this practice, Paul says we must come to the Word and wash ourselves in the Word of God before we can be sanctified, before we can enter into the Holy of Holies, before we can live for Jesus.

After you are saved, you need the everlasting fountain of truth in Scripture to cleanse you day by day, moment by moment, morning by morning, and evening by evening. You need to have the source of truth running in you and running through you. The Word of God is that fountain. It is our source of all truth.

Every Sunday before reading the Scripture at the start of my sermon, I remind the congregation of this source of truth by saying, “This is the Word of God.” We position the pulpit in the center of the platform and we elevate it because we teach and preach that the Word of God is the source of all truth. While we need to argue against untruth with people in the world, we in our churches never need to argue what is truth because we have the source of truth.

THE STUDY OF TRUTH

Not only is the Bible the source of truth, it is also the study of truth. In John 8:31, Jesus says we are to abide, to live, or to remain in the Word. In 2 Timothy 2:15, Paul admonishes his young disciple Timothy to,

> Be diligent to present yourself approved to God as a workman who does not need to be ashamed, handling accurately the Word of truth.

An unread Bible is like delicious food uneaten. It is like a love letter unopened. It is like gold that has never been mined. It is like a sword that is never unsheathed. Every believer needs to read the Bible. Proverbs 23:23 commands us to,

> Buy truth, and do not sell it.

The Bible was the first book ever published on the printing press. It remains the number one bestseller.[2] Today portions of the Bible have been translated into more than 2400 languages around the world—still not nearly enough to reach readers throughout the globe.[3]

There are now over 30 different English translations of the Word of God.[4] In America we have Bibles "running out our ears" as we used to say back home. Sadly, we don't get the Scripture into our hearts because American Christians as a group are lazy and never take time to read the Bible—the Word of God.

Every graduating high school senior should be given a copy of the book, *The New Evidence That Demands a Verdict* by Josh McDowell. Two of the high school graduates who received copies at our church called me after going to their classes at a very large state university.

Both their phone calls went something like this:

"Pastor, I'm in this biology class, and you were right—my faith is being challenged. They're telling me I came from ooze rather than from God. Then I have a guy over here telling me the Bible's not the Word of God. How do I know if it is?"

I asked, "Do you have your copy of *The New Evidence That Demands a Verdict*?"

"Well, no, sir. I left it in Pensacola."

I replied, "Don't call me again until you go home and get your book. Dig it out for yourself. Study the Bible. Use those three brain cells you have! Rub them together and get truth into your head!"

We must use our minds. God has called all of His children to add knowledge to their moral excellence. We need not only to believe the Bible is truth, but we also need to know why the Bible is authoritative.

Josh McDowell delineates eleven assertions about the uniqueness of the Bible.

"The Bible is the only book that was…

1. Written over about a fifteen-hundred-year span

2. Written by more than forty authors from every walk of life, including kings, military leaders, peasants, philosophers, fishermen, tax collectors, poets, musicians, statesmen, scholars, and shepherds. For example:

    Moses, a political leader and judge, trained in the universities of Egypt;
    David, a king, poet, musician, shepherd, and warrior;
    Amos, a herdsman;

Joshua, a military general;
Nehemiah, a cupbearer to a pagan king;
Daniel, a prime minister;
Solomon, a king and philosopher;
Luke, a physician and historian;
Peter, a fisherman;
Matthew, a tax collector;
Paul, a rabbi; and
Mark, Peter's secretary.

3. Written in different places:
   By Moses in the wilderness,
   Jeremiah in a dungeon,
   Daniel on a hillside and in a palace,
   Paul inside prison walls,
   Luke while traveling
   John while in exile on the isle of Patmos.

4. Written at different times:
   David in times of war and sacrifice
   Solomon in times of peace and prosperity.

5. Written during different moods:
   Some writing from the heights of joy;
   Others writing from the depths of sorrow and despair;
   Some during times of certainty and conviction;
   Others during days of confusion and doubt.

6. Written on three continents:
   Asia
   Africa
   Europe.

7. Written in three languages:
   Hebrew…
   Aramaic…
   Greek….

8. Written in a wide variety of literary styles, including: poetry, historical narrative, song, romance, didactic treatise, personal correspondence, memoirs, satire, biography, autobiography, law, prophecy, parable, and allegory.

9. The Bible addresses hundreds of controversial subjects...[and] hundreds of hot topics (e.g. marriage, divorce and remarriage, homosexuality, adultery, obedience to authority, truth-telling and lying, character development, parenting, the nature and revelation of God)….with an amazing degree of harmony.

10. In spite of its diversity, the Bible presents a single unfolding story: God's redemption of human beings.

11. Finally, and most important, among all the people described in the Bible, the leading character throughout is the one, true, living God made known through Jesus Christ."[5]

In 1 Peter 3:15 Peter exhorts us to,

> …sanctify Christ as Lord in your hearts, always being ready to make a defense to everyone who asks you to give an account for the hope that is in you….

The Greek word for this type of hope is *apologia* from which we get our English word *apologetics*. This does not mean we apologize. It means we give a reason—a defense—for our belief in Jesus Christ and His Word. Our belief must not be based on how we feel. Our actions must not be predicated on feeling. We must come to the place of knowing truth, and that truth is not what we feel. The facts of reality must line up with truth. The facts of reality are that God so loved the world He gave His Son. God gave us His book of truth, and we need to be studying that book, carrying out Paul's admonition to handle the Word of God with accuracy. We must be historically accurate, contextually true, and grammatically precise. We must study truth found in the Holy Scriptures.

I want to present a challenge to all men who are sports nuts like me. In the next year, read the Bible the same number of hours you spend watching sports on television. For me that means in the fall, each time my football team plays a three-hour long game, I owe God three hours in the Word. And if they go into overtime, so do I. If you are a golfer who can calculate a handicap, you can read the book of John. Read the Bible!

I'm amazed that Christians will watch the evening news at 5:00, 6:00, and 10:00—the *same* news all three times. To those of you who love the news, I want to ask you to read the Bible as much as you listen to the news on television. If you are going to give the local newscaster an hour and a half a day, shouldn't you give the Lord Jesus the same amount of time?

Most people simply don't want to know what the Bible says. When people tell me they can't understand the Bible, I counter by saying they can understand this book if they will read it and keep reading it until they *do* understand.

Study the Word of God. The Bible is not beyond comprehension; understanding begins with reading. Acquire a study Bible and add some good study books. Because God has called us to have knowledge of Him, we must become students of His Word.

THE STRENGTH OF TRUTH

We have examined the source of truth and the study of truth, and now consider the strength of truth. Jesus said if you abide in His word, it proves you are His disciple (John 8:31). You will know the truth and the truth will set you free (John 8:32). Jesus rules the church, and the Scripture is the scepter by which He rules. He rules with the Word of God. When He rules your life, He does not bring oppression. He brings liberation. Freedom results when truth comes into your life. There are four areas where Jesus will set you free.

You can be free from tradition

The Bible teaches us that Jesus will set us free from tradition. Jesus is speaking about the tradition of the scribes and Pharisees in Mark 7:8-9.

> Neglecting the commandment of God, you hold to the tradition of men. You nicely set aside the commandment of God in order to keep your tradition.

They chose to forsake God's direction for man's inclination. If we are not careful, we will be just like the scribes and Pharisees. We will set aside the authority of God and pick up our own practices. Tradition always wants us to *look* right rather than *be* right. Tradition says dress right, sit correctly, always look the part of a good church member.

Some parents don't want their sons to have an earring because it doesn't look right. I concur. I'm not giving license to it. I don't want it at my house! But did you know a man can have an earring and still be right—can still be a godly man? You can have traditional, good-looking ears and have a very dark, ungodly heart. Tradition deals with the outward look, and unfortunately, we often would rather be right before everybody else rather than seek to be right before God.

I have a dear friend who is a marvelous evangelist. He has two sons. One son is clean-cut and looks like the all-American boy. Any dad would be delighted to have that young man come to his house to date his daughter. Then there is the other son—tattoos all over and piercings everywhere. I finally asked my friend, "How do you deal with that?"

His response was a shock. The son that doesn't *look* right *is* right! He is living in a different culture, winning men and women to faith in Jesus Christ and reaching people that no one else will be able to reach. My friend told me he doesn't like what his son looks like nor the way the church responds to his boy's looks, but he had to come to understand that the Holy Spirit was accurate when He helped write the Old Testament. God looks not on the outside but looks on the inside (1 Samuel 16:7).

FREE YOURSELF FROM TRADITION

Tradition only looks outwardly to judge a person. God's eyes see us from His exclusive inside view. Let me hasten to say that when a person gets right with God on the inside, it does affect the way he or she looks on the outside in dress and demeanor. Modesty and decency should be evident in the lives of those pursuing Christ. But we must be careful not to interject tradition as a sign of godliness.

You can be free from the world's lies

The truth of God will give you freedom from the world's lies. In Romans 1:25, the Bible says "they exchanged the truth of God for a lie." One of the world's lies says jealousy and selfish ambition are the ways of life. But the Bible commands us to serve others and not ourselves. The Word of God—when you come to understand truth—will set you free from jealousy and selfish ambition.

Most of us want our kids to be successful to make us look good. When the world presents the suave and handsome rich man as the paragon of success, we must counter with God's truth. According to Psalm 139, God created each of us just as we are, and that makes each of His creations a success. If you always wanted a six-foot-two, barrel-chested son who could sing, but instead you got a skinny boy who loves computers, you have to love him. What we must do is come to the place that we accept our kids just the way God gave them to us. Fathers are not very good at that. When we come to understand the truth of the Word of God, we will understand that God never made a mistake when He created our children. Dad, when you and I receive the truth that God is in creation, then the truth of the Word will set you free.

ABANDON THE WORLD'S LIES

Not everyone knows this, but I have had two sons. I had one boy until he turned thirteen, and then I found he had changed into a "new" son. God made him one way for thirteen years just to test me. That's right. It was all for me. I didn't know what to do. I just had to say, "God, I take him just as he is." Then something happened. He went through a change in his life, and now he is as good a friend as I have in the world today. He's my buddy. We hang out together. We laugh a lot. I learned I had to love them both.

Dad—hear me! The truth of God will set you free when you begin to understand God made your children just the way they are. You'd better get on with loving them and helping them understand the way God has called them to be. Let God's truth sink into you, knowing that He has all things under His control. You can trust Him, and when you do, He will set you free. If you want a ballplayer and you get a band member, get happy! If you have a ballplayer and you want a band member, get happy! Trust God to set you free from the world's lie that your kids have to be a certain way to be classified as an achievement in your eyes.

You can be free from personal ignorance

Not only does the Word of God set you free from tradition and worldly lies, it will set you free from personal ignorance. For example, it's amazing what Christians believe as truth that is actually not in the Bible. It's astounding what we believe about the devil that's not in the Bible.

Many Christians will tell you Satan is in charge of hell. That is not biblical. The devil is not in charge of hell. Artists draw cartoons that place St. Peter at the gate of heaven and depict the devil sitting on a throne in hell scheming his evil plots. The Bible says Satan is going to be cast into hell. He is not there now. He doesn't possess the keys or dominion over hell. He is not the prince of Hades. God is in charge of eternity, not the old wicked one.

TRUTH OVERCOMES IGNORANCE

Some people think that Satan is everywhere, but the devil has never been omnipresent. The devil does not mirror Jehovah God. He is merely a fallen angel. The devil mirrors Michael, the archangel.

Most of us think Satan is the source of all temptation in our lives, but he is not. Sometimes *you* are the source of your temptation, for out of your own selfish, fleshly desires you go after things you know shouldn't be in your life. The devil doesn't have to bother with you because you are already caught in the snares of the world and the flesh. We give Satan way too much credit. You see, the scenario is not the devil on one side and God on the other, fighting it out as if they are co-equal. There is just one God, Jehovah is His name, and He is the victor. He has been the winner all along. If you will simply read the Bible, the Scripture will set you free from personal ignorance.

You can be free from spiritual bondage

Lastly, the Word of God will set you free from spiritual bondage. So many people find themselves under spiritual oppression. They come into the church, walk down the aisle, receive Christ as Savior, take the preacher by the hand, and suddenly think they now have to live like Mr. Deacon, Mrs. Preacher's Wife, or Miss Saint. They place themselves in bondage to an expectation. I once counseled a man who used to be in the church, but no longer attended. He used to be a tither, but was no longer giving. He used to be a worker, but was no longer involved.

FACTUAL FAITH MUST SUPERSEDE FEELINGS

I asked, "What happened?"

He replied, "I lost my job, and when I couldn't give, I thought I lost the capability and the responsibility and the ability to have a voice in the church because I didn't have anything to give. Then some people ostracized me and did some things I think were wrong. Am I right or am I wrong?"

I said, "Yes, sir. You're right and you're wrong. You're wrong to believe that giving money validates your ability to serve in the church. Some people don't have any money. You don't, and you don't have a job. How can you give if you have nothing?

He said, "Yeah, but I just feel…"

"Quit feeling and come to a factual faith," I retorted. "God will give you the feeling you need only through obedience. And, yes, you are right. If you were ostracized, the church was in error and we failed, but we love you, and I want you to know there's a place for you to serve. When God blesses you, you give as you can. When He gives you ability, you serve."

Then the proverbial light bulb came on. He said, "Is that right?"

"I told you it was, didn't I? Have I ever told you anything that wasn't true? Do you think I'd lie to you?"

"I don't think you would."

"No, sir, I wouldn't. I'm telling you the truth."

That day the man was released from spiritual bondage based upon feelings and restored to a factual faith. When you make your heart right with God, He'll set you free from the bondage that the spirit of this world wants to place upon you. First, come by faith and be saved, and then begin to learn moral excellence. It is through the washing of the water from the Word of God that we are sanctified. And through knowledge God creates holiness in our lives. We must apply to our faith moral excellence and live holy lives by the truth of God. In the octave of our spiritual development, too many of us are missing the "tone" of sanctification that comes from knowledge of the Word of God.

OUR THIRD NOTE IS GOD'S CALL TO SANCTIFICATION

Every believer should live life by a creed that reads like this: I believe the Word of God. I believe all of it. I submit to its authority. I pledge to study it diligently. I pledge to obey it fully. God loves me and I love Him. I will take His direction to heart, be obedient to Him, and go where He tells me to go. I believe the Word of God. Hallelujah! Hallelujah! Hallelujah!

REPEAT

1. List the eight callings of God found in 2 Peter 1:5-7.

   ____

   ____

   ____

   ____

   ____

   ____

   ____

   ____

2. Knowledge is the calling to ______________________.

3. What is an agnostic?

4. What is an atheist?

5. What does *sanctify* mean?

6. Identify each of the following:

    The person of truth

    The place of truth

    The page of truth

INTERPRET

7. Explain how the Bible is our source of all truth.

8. Describe how studying the Word of God can free you from the following:

    Tradition

    The world's lies

    Personal ignorance

    Spiritual bondage

9. In addition to reading your Bible diligently and daily, how can you increase your knowledge of God's Word?

10. How can increasing in the knowledge of the Bible lead to moral excellence and sanctified living?

PRACTICE

11. What do you plan to do to abide in God's Word?

12. How do you plan to develop skill in "handling accurately" the Word of God?

13. If it is your desire to do so, copy the creed at the end of this chapter and make it your way of life.

PAUSE

Father, thank You for giving us Your Word. I ask that You grant me knowledge of the truth of Jesus Christ found in Your Word. May I experience the freedom such knowledge brings. Make me a positive influence for You, God, not bound by legalism, tradition, or spiritual bondage. I believe and submit to the authority of Your Word. In the holy name of Jesus, I pray. Amen.

4
The Calling of *Service*

In 2 Peter 1:5-7, God has given us precious and magnificent promises. He says that we are to be growing believers. Just as the eight notes of an octave achieve the desired result of beautiful music, the eight parts of our calling are arranged so that we accomplish the goal of becoming more like our Lord Jesus Christ. The first note is

FAITH, and add to your faith
MORAL EXCELLENCE, to your moral excellence add
KNOWLEDGE, to your knowledge add
SELF-CONTROL, to your self-control add
PERSEVERANCE, to your perseverance add
GODLINESS, to your godliness add
BROTHERLY KINDNESS, and to your brotherly kindness add
LOVE.

SELF-CONTROL IS THE CALL TO SERVICE

Many Christians play only three notes of the octave. Those three notes are just enough to perform the opening phrase of "Three Blind Mice"! God wants all the notes of the octave to be in your life so you can sing the songs of the Lord with gusto. We have considered *faith*, the calling of salvation; *moral excellence*, the calling of separation; *knowledge*, the calling of sanctification; and now we consider *self-control*, the calling of service.

Reading and applying 1 Corinthians 9 will help us add self-control to our lives.

> Do you not know that those who run in a race all run, but only one receives the prize? Run in such a way that you may win. And everyone who competes in the games exercises self-control in all things. They then do it to receive a perishable wreath, but we an imperishable. Therefore I run in such a way, as not without aim; I box in such a way, as not beating the air; but I buffet my body and make it my slave, lest possibly, after I have preached to others, I myself should be disqualified.

Paul is alluding to the Isthmian Games that took place in Corinth, Greece during his century. We can compare them to the Olympic Games of today.

In the Winter Olympics, we see the athletes ski, sled and skate for that top honor of winning the gold medal in their sport. In summer, they run, vault, and swim. The competitions are numerous and the preparation is extensive. Athletes discipline themselves and prepare for years. They are all there competing because they have exercised self-control. Self-control is the ability to make the right decision even when it contradicts our desires. Those who win in the Christian life will understand and exercise self-control.

SELF-CONTROL ENABLES RIGHT DECISIONS

Self-control is not the same as being in control. Self-control is the ability to control our flesh and its desires and exercise God's principles in life. Only God can bring us to that place and it is a process. If you think you will simply say, "I'm going to answer the call of service and add self-control to my life," you will fall flat in your pursuit. You must begin with faith and moral excellence and have knowledge before you will ever be able to exercise self-control.

Notice again the example of that ancient runner in the Isthmian Games. He is training to become the fastest runner. There would have been days when he did not want to get up from his sleeping pallet, but he had self-control to get up anyway. There would have been days when he wanted to eat things that were not on his training program, but he had the self-control to say "no" to that second raisin cake or third fig bar. Why? Because he was willing to train in such a way so he might win.

FAITH,
MORAL EXCELLENCE,
AND
KNOWLEDGE
ARE STEPS TO
SELF-CONTROL

Everyone who has this kind of commitment will exercise self-control. Those first century athletes competed for a perishable wreath—no medals, just a simple loop of laurel leaves. But as God's "runners" we are running in such a way that we may win an imperishable crown from our Lord. Therefore, we bring our bodies under self-discipline so that we can win the race set before us.

THE STRUGGLE FOR SELF-CONTROL

There is no doubt about it—we face a struggle for self-control. The Bible says in 1Thessalonians 5:23,

> Now may the God of peace Himself sanctify you entirely; and may your spirit and soul and body be preserved complete, without blame at the coming of our Lord Jesus Christ.

It was Paul's prayer that as believers we would be sanctified entirely in our body, soul, and spirit. Everyone knows what Paul meant by the body. The body is our flesh. We all have one. Some of us have more of one than we want, and some of us have less. But if you do not have a body, then you are dead and have already gone to heaven. Since you are obviously still here, be sanctified in your body.

YOUR CONSCIENCE NEEDS TO INFLUENCE YOUR MIND, WILL, AND EMOTIONS

Then Paul says to be sanctified in your soul. Your soul is your mind, will, and emotions. You are sanctified in your spirit at salvation when God quickens your spirit and makes you alive with Christ, rescued from spiritual death. Your sanctified spirit now needs to influence your mind, will, and emotions.

Your spirit may be more recognizable to you when it is identified as your conscience. Evangelist Junior Hill defined the conscience as the moral standard God has endowed to believers so they may know right from wrong. The conscience is designed to bear witness to your mind, will, and emotions. The conscience of a believer is clarified by the truth of Scripture and becomes pure and clean and undefiled. It will temper the mind (where we think), the will (where we decide), and the emotions (where we feel).

No one likes to struggle, but sanctification usually requires us to combat the strength of self in all areas of our lives. It is in those last two areas—the most fervent parts of our lives—where we face our biggest struggle with self-control.

We struggle with our will

One of our most difficult challenges is in the area of the will. We want to do what we want to do, regardless of how much we want to live a sanctified life. Many times we err by rationalizing wrong actions that come out of that struggle. When we rationalize a wrong action, we beat down and dull the conscience. This precludes character from guiding us. When the conscience becomes deadened, it can no longer restrain our fervent, ungodly desires. Two things happen: (1) we do not exhibit self-control, but instead we (2) embrace will-control. And when the will is in control of your life, you end up throwing a tantrum.

When I was growing up, my dad made me cut the grass. I hated mowing the grass. We had acres of it. The day I left for college, he purchased a riding mower, but I had to use the old push kind (and it was not self-propelled). I would procrastinate and put it off and wait until it was late in the day. Finally, I started cutting that grass. There were days when I was so rebellious in my soul that I would run that lawn mower into a tree over and over again. My will was completely out of control and I pitched a marvelous hissy-fit! Have you ever had one?

Recently I boarded a flight to Atlanta. I was seated in a row with a married couple. An elderly woman of Indian descent sat in the row in front of us, and next to her was a woman who appeared to be in her twenties and was probably her daughter. They were speaking to each other in their native language, and I could not understand a word. They had a little boy with them who was about two—cute as a button but wild as a billy goat. He was screaming at the top of his lungs. Every time his mother told him something, he would scream. It was so shrill it hurt my ears. It hurt ears ten rows up and ten rows back. People were standing up and turning around to see where the yelling was coming from. Their facial expressions manifested the collective thought, "Somebody control that kid!"

The child continued screaming and screaming and screaming. Twice the man next to me stood up, leaned over to the woman, and said, "Somebody get this boy under control!" I was sitting there writing a sermon titled "The Calling of Service: Understanding Self-Control," when I said to myself, *Uh-oh—somebody better get* him *under control.*

We were about fifteen minutes out of Atlanta, the little boy was still screaming and bouncing up and down, when all of a sudden my seatmate had had all he could stand. He began to kick the back of the child's seat. I don't mean he kicked it once. I don't mean he kicked it five times. He kept kicking and kicking and kicking. Finally one of the flight attendants came to him and announced that a sky marshal would be meeting us at the gate. I thought to myself, *Here's a man in his mid-thirties having a tantrum on an airplane.* His will was totally out of control.

TANTRUMS ARE SIN AGAINST GOD

Even a Christian's will sometimes gets out of control and he will have a tantrum. Some people justify themselves by saying, "Well, my kids are just that way," or "That boy is hurting my ears, therefore I can kick him out of the seat." No, that is not an excuse for lack of control of the will. We must not rationalize away our conscience and allow "will-control" to take over. The truth is that when we throw tantrums, we are sinning against God. When that man kicked the little boy's seat for about the twentieth time, the mother stood and spoke her first English word on that flight. She began to protect her son.

I was sitting there wondering, *What should I do? I'm afraid I'm going to be a witness for the prosecution in some lawsuit, and I don't want to be a witness.* So I pretended to be asleep, though nobody could have been sleeping with all that "turbulence" going on. As I mentally continued my sermon preparation with my eyes closed, I concluded that when the will is out of control, there will always be a struggle. And if we are totally honest, learning self-control is difficult for us all, but we can find victory!

We struggle with our emotions

When the will gets out of control, it leads to a tantrum. When emotions get out of control, it leads to insatiable lust. Lust is not just a sexual emotion. That is the main connotation, but only a fraction of the full meaning. Greed will enter. Anger will enter. Unforgiveness will enter the picture when emotion is out of control.

The story of a young man who played football for a Midwestern university flew across America on the Internet, and many publications picked up the headline. After practice one day the young man went to a drive-through at a nearby fast food chain and ordered several items. When his order was handed to him, he discovered that they had left a chalupa out of his bag. The football player lost control. He got out of his car and started to climb through the window to get his missing food and exact his revenge on the delinquent fast food employee. About thirty minutes later, the paramedics arrived to extract the six foot three, 260-pound young man who had gotten himself trapped. He could get through the window, but he could not get out. He was stuck in the drive-up window at Taco Bell.

You may not have been a project for your local paramedics, but have you ever had your emotions get out of control when you were not served the way you thought you should have been served? Once again, the struggle for your self-control ensues and your witness for Christ is in jeopardy.

The Bible says to add self-control to your knowledge. When our wills are uncontrolled and our emotions are unrestrained, we become undisciplined rather than retaining self-control. And when we get out of control, our testimonies are totally ineffective. The football player may have been a Christian, but to the people he encountered that night, his actions negated his witness. We can empathize, however, because we all struggle with self-control of our emotions.

In Acts 24:16, Paul has just been arrested. His Jewish opponents are demanding that he answer their accusations against him in front of Festus, the Roman king. In his reply Paul states,

> I also do my best to maintain always a blameless conscience both before God and before men.

Paul is saying that he strives to stay faultless before men and before God. If our conscience is to be clean, our struggle is not only in allowing God to be in control, but we will also struggle with maintaining a clear conscience with mankind. When we don't forgive and won't forget, and when we become angry with others, we cannot uphold self-control. Consequently, we cannot safeguard a clean, pure conscience with others, nor will we have an untainted conscience before the Lord. Paul said he is doing his best. He is striving, and this is his struggle—the struggle for self-control. We all share it, do we not? We all share that struggle because our wills and our emotions are difficult to control.

THE DEVELOPMENT OF SELF-CONTROL BY THE SPIRIT

Because God lives in us as believers, we have the ability to produce the fruit of the Spirit. One of the nine fruits of the Spirit is self-control.

Galatians 5:22-23 says,

> But the fruit of the Spirit is love, joy, peace, patience, kindness, goodness, faithfulness, gentleness, self-control; against such things there is no law.

If you are a Christian, right now you have a conscience that is either clear by living up to the principles of Christ (1 Timothy 3:9), or you have a seared conscience caused by giving into sinful living (1 Timothy 4:2). The seared conscience has no feeling. Therefore your mind, will, and emotions are not tempered by your conscience. Your conscience has been numbed by your own corrupt acts. According to 1 Timothy 1:5,

> The goal of our instruction is love from a pure heart and a good conscience and a sincere faith.

But notice the warning found in Titus 1:15.

> To the pure, all things are pure; but to those who are defiled and unbelieving, nothing is pure, but both their mind and their conscience are defiled.

When believers think like the world and the culture they live in, their consciences are corrupted. Consider again the example of abortion. This world says abortion is a means of birth control; therefore, abortion is not sin. And if we are not careful, we as Christians begin to think like the world thinks. Our consciences may become so defiled that if our own daughter becomes pregnant out of wedlock, we decide it must be acceptable for her to have an abortion because the world says it is. But a clean, clear, pure, blameless conscience says, "What does the Word of God say?" The Word of God calls it murder.

A BLAMELESS CONSCIENCE SEEKS THE WORD OF GOD

We must decide: will our consciences be clean and clear, or will they be seared and defiled? Only when we allow the Spirit of God living within us to have total control can we experience a life of *divinely driven self-control.*

There are six actions you must take if you are going to successfully walk with God and achieve self-control.

- **Give up control**
- **Ask for forgiveness**
- **Flee temptation**
- **Adopt high standards**
- **Resist the "bait"**
- **Be utterly enthralled with Jesus**

The first thing you must do is *give up control.* Today a favorite "toy" among men is the remote control. Most of us have half a dozen in our homes. You have to surrender the remote control of your life and place it in the hand of God. You begin by saying, "Lord, I am no longer in charge. I give control to You. I am not the Lord of my life. I am not the master of my way." You must confirm that God is in control.

You have to abandon that desire to be in command of your life. Hand over control to the Father.

Second, you have to *ask forgiveness* of those you have offended. You will never have a clean conscience until you say, "I was wrong. I'm sorry." The only way to get your conscience clear is to go and deal with the people you have wronged. Some of you have so wronged your children that you need to ask their forgiveness. You have not only hurt your conscience, but you have hurt theirs. Many middle-aged adults are still being ruled by their parents. Some of you are still being governed by your parents who have been dead and gone for years. They control you from the grave. You can't seem to relinquish some things they said to you or move beyond past hurts they caused. Even though you may have been deeply injured, you must forgive them and "forget" their erroneous teaching. You must choose not to dwell on the past and choose to forgive.

Third, *flee temptation.* The Word of God tells us to flee youthful lust, to run away from temptation. When you see it coming, turn and run! Dr. Tommy Turner spoke at one of our men's retreats and said to us, "Every temptation comes with a small window of decision time." We may get a half-second, a second and a half, or three seconds before temptation sets in. An inappropriate program begins on television. We may glance at that magazine on the news rack. A tantalizing thought slips in. But we all have that window of opportunity. We will either flee or we will forge a relationship with that sin. We must learn to escape from harmful temptation. Flee!

SELF-CONTROL FLEES TEMPTATION

After you give up control, ask forgiveness, and flee temptation, number four is *adopt high standards.* If you are going to have self-control, you have to make up your mind you are going to win before you get in the war! You have to decide which way you will go and whose standards you will follow *before* temptation arises. Make it your objective to adopt the highest standards—those found in the Word of God.

Many of the teenagers in our churches have made a True Love Waits commitment. They have adopted the standard to remain sexually pure until marriage. That is a very high and worthy standard. Is that a foolproof way to retain self-control? No, it is not foolproof. Each teen must personally say with his lips that true love waits. But as he or she is faced with high-pressure dating temptations, each must answer the question, "What am I going to do with my hands and eyes and actions now?" But we should set the benchmark high and pursue standards of biblical proportions.

Number five: *resist the bait.* This world is tossing enticements out to us all the time, trying to provoke us to succumb to temptation. Magazines, television, videos, the Internet, and a thousand other things persistently grasp at our attention. The lure of sin is all around the believer. We must learn to refuse to take the bait.

Finally, *be utterly enthralled with Jesus!* We have to be in love with Jesus more than we are in love with anything in this world or we will never come to the place of having self-control.

Self-control is not an easy part of the Christian life. It is not easy for me. There are times when my emotions and my will want to take over, but when I have given God control and walked with these six disciplines, my standards are set and I can flee temptation. I want to find myself in love with the Lord Jesus every waking moment. Then I find that I can embrace self-control.

Why did Paul use an athletic illustration for self-control? I know why. Self-control is displayed so significantly by the example of athletes. You can't survive the discipline that participation in athletics requires unless you have self-control.

In the Christian life, the Spirit of God lives within you and will encourage you, energize you, and help you to sustain self-control.

THE OUTCOME OF GOD'S CONTROL: SERVICE

You may be asking, "What has self-control got to do with service?" This is the connection. If *you* are in control, that power in your life will lead to selfishness. But when God is in control and you allow Him to control your mind, will, and emotions, then you are released to do service.

In Galatians 5:13, before Paul writes about the fruit of the Spirit, he refers to self-control.

> For you were called to freedom, brethren; only do not turn your freedom into an opportunity for the flesh, but through love serve one another.

After you are saved, you have been set free, but you are not free to do anything you want. When Paul speaks of the flesh, he means your mind, will, and emotions. You and your flesh are free in Christ, but do not let your freedom lead you to believe that since you are forgiven, you can do anything you wish. Our freedom leads us to service. As Paul dictates, through love we are to serve one another.

THE UNSELFISHNESS OF A GOD-CONTROLLED BELIEVER LEADS TO SERVICE

You see, as you develop self-control, you grow into a *bondservant* to Christ as demonstrated in Exodus 21. In this Old Testament passage, when a Jewish bondslave had worked out his indenture, he could choose freedom or choose to become a permanent servant to his master. If he chose to stay, his ear was pierced with an awl against the doorpost signifying his commitment to remain with his master and become a bondservant. Out of our free volition, we also must decide to become a bondservant of God and choose to serve Him as Master and Lord.

I believe *the greatest service is serving children.* From the Galatians 5:13 passage we receive the admonition to be loving servants. Why do I believe serving kids is the most important service we can do? Two reasons. First, most people who make a decision to follow Christ do so under the age of eighteen. If you reach the age of eighteen and you are not a Christian, it is very unlikely you will ever be saved. Young hearts are much more pliable. A child's heart finds it simple to love God and open up to Him. A child says, "Jesus, come into my heart" and means just what he says.

The second reason why it is so important to serve kids is because most often God places His call to ministry on someone's life in their childhood. I was twelve years old when I heard the call of God for the first time. Brother Banks was preaching about the call to ministry. I was one of those kids who sit in the back filling in all the circles in the bulletin, when suddenly the Spirit of God—as we used to say—"grabbed a-hold of me". I looked up and thought, *I think I'm going to do that. I'm going to answer God's call.* It was the first time I ever felt a stirring in my spirit. It did not come to fruition until I was seventeen, but it began when my heart was young.

Preschoolers who have a happy time at church want to keep coming to Sunday School. Many career missionaries were called by God while attending Girls in Action, Royal Ambassadors, and Mission Friends. We must never underestimate the importance of serving children.

Zechariah 8:5 says,

> And the streets of the city [New Jerusalem] will be filled with boys and girls playing in its streets.

Serving children will be rewarding and inspiring as you literally impact the future. Are you looking for something to fulfill your life? Serve! And the greatest place to serve is with children.

If you can say "no" to serving children, then one of two things is real in your life. Either God has not called you to serve children (He doesn't call everybody, but He does call many) or you are so in control of your own life that you cannot hear the call of God to service. Until you have self-control, you will never serve in kingdom work here on earth. But when God is in you and He is in control, you will become a loving servant-hearted laborer for Christ.

THE GREATEST SERVICE IS SERVING CHILDREN

When I think about the people in my life who were influencers as I was growing up, I always think of my basketball coach. He was like a father to me. Coach Cooley was quite rugged and spoke some rough language, but what a guy! He's dead now, and I still miss him.

I think of Mr. Gamble, our Sunday School teacher. We met in an old, wood-framed house across the street from the church. It was like a big tree house and was cold in the winter and hot in the summer, but we loved it. Our sixth grade class met upstairs and we would hang out there, bring our pocket knives and carve on the walls. I can still hear old Mr. Gamble say, "Cut that out and open up your Bibles." We secretly laughed at the pun while we obeyed and put our knives away.

Then they moved us across the street to the cinder block building and Mr. Kenimer was our teacher. I can still remember the smell of that Sunday School room. It reeked of mildew and was the stinkiest place I had ever been, but Mr. Kenimer loved us and we knew it.

Shorty was our RA director. He couldn't find Genesis or Matthew if his life depended on it. *We* knew more Bible than he did when he took on our class. But there was something about the way that guy loved us. When you were around Shorty, he would always give you a hug and rub you on the head. He began to learn the Bible, and he taught it to us.

As I think back, these were my influencers. Mrs. Gant was also one of these. The night she died, I was at her home and watched them roll her body out on the stretcher. I would miss her. When I was seventeen, Mr. Claude Wheeler taught me to be a soul winner. He showed me how to mark my New Testament to be a more effective witness.

Liz and I were really busy one year during the Christmas season, and as a result we sent out our Christmas cards late. One day shortly after, I received a note back from Mrs. Katie Wright, who lived in a senior adult facility. With an obviously shaky hand, Miss Katie wrote, "Thank you for the card and family picture. I thought I wasn't going to get one this year." She continued, "I prayed for you when you were a boy."

Many years ago when I went forward in church to announce my call to preach, Miss Katie came through the line to shake my hand. This bondservant of the Most High God took me by the hand and said, "Ted, God told me six years ago you were going to be a preacher. I've been waiting on this day."

I said, "Well, Miss Katie, why didn't you tell me?"

She replied, "Oh, no, son. If you can't hear God call you to preach, you'll never hear Him call you to pastor a church." I believe she was still praying for me until the day she died.

These were not master theologians. They were bondservants. These were not people with tons of money. They were bondservants. These were people with self-control. They were unashamedly committed to Jesus. Perfect? Goodness, no! They simply lived under the control of the Master, serving kids like me.

We need great children's ministries in all our churches. We must pile resources and place tremendous efforts into these ministries. We must have loyal men with self-control serving in the children's divisions of our churches. Why? Because millions and millions of boys and girls living in America today do not know their biological fathers. Countless numbers live in every city and town. They need a daddy. They need the influence of a godly man. They need a bondservant to love them—and we must do it. We must be a family to these children and lead them to Christ. Say "Yes, Lord," to service for the kingdom's sake. Add to your

> SELF-CONTROL, WHICH IS THE CALL TO SERVICE, IS OUR FOURTH NOTE

FAITH

MORAL EXCELLENCE, to your moral excellence

KNOWLEDGE, and to your knowledge add

SELF-CONTROL.

Commit your life to the Lordship of Christ.

REPEAT

1. List the first four of the eight callings of God

   The call to…
   ______________________________, which is the call to______________________________

   The call to…
   ______________________________, which is the call to______________________________

   The call to…
   ______________________________, which is the call to______________________________

   The call to…
   ______________________________, which is the call to______________________________

2. List the remaining four callings of God.

   ____

   ____

   ____

   ____

3. In 1 Corinthians 9:24-27, what athletic event is Paul referring to?

4. In what three areas of our lives are we to be sanctified?

5. We know what the body is; how would you define the soul and the spirit?

INTERPRET

6. How does one deaden his conscience?

7. What is the relationship between self-control and service?

8. Why is it so important to have a dynamic program for our children?

PRACTICE

9. Is there someone you need to forgive or something you need to forget? Will you plan to make things right with others and with God? Write down when and how you plan to do this.

10. In what areas of your life is your self-control weak? What is your specific plan for strengthening these weaknesses?

11. Does God want you to serve in a children's ministry? What may He be calling you to do? What spiritual gifts, talents, or aptitudes do you have that you can use in this ministry?

12. Is there an influencer in your life whom you could delight with a thank-you note or card expressing gratitude? Send it, for that person's sake and for your own.

PAUSE

Father, my prayer is that I become a growing believer. Bring me to self-control over my flesh so that I may exercise Your principles in my life. I ask that the Spirit develop such fruit in my life that I will be a pleasing witness of You. Empower me to flee temptation and to forgive those I have wronged. I offer myself as a bondservant to Your Lordship. In Your name, Lord, I pray. Amen.

5
The Calling of *Suffering*

In 2 Peter 1:5-7, we have been examining practices we must add to our faith so that our lives are in agreement with God's will. Just as we practice our skills in music, we must also sharpen our spiritual talents. First, we are called to salvation with faith. With our

FAITH we are to add
MORAL EXCELLENCE, to our moral excellence add
KNOWLEDGE, to our knowledge add
SELF-CONTROL; now we are ready to add to our abilities
PERSEVERANCE. Then we will add
BROTHERLY KINDNESS, and finally
LOVE.

PERSEVERANCE IS THE CALL TO SUFFERING

As we continue to see how we may learn to live in harmony with Christ, let's look at 1 Peter 4:12-19 and then discover why I call perseverance the calling of suffering.

> Beloved, do not be surprised at the fiery ordeal among you, which comes upon you for your testing, as though some strange thing were happening to you; but to the degree that you share the sufferings of Christ, keep on

> rejoicing; so that also at the revelation of His glory, you may rejoice with exultation. If you are reviled for the name of Christ, you are blessed, because the Spirit of glory and of God rests upon you. By no means let any of you suffer as a murderer, or thief, or evildoer, or a troublesome meddler; but if anyone suffers as a Christian, let him not feel ashamed, but in that name let him glorify God. For it is time for judgment to begin with the household of God; and if it begins with us first, what will be the outcome for those who do not obey the gospel of God? And if it is with difficulty that the righteous is saved, what will become of the godless man and the sinner? Therefore, let those also who suffer according to the will of God entrust their souls to a faithful Creator in doing what is right.

I was once in a worship service and heard a lady say, "You cannot have a testimony without a test." When the tests come, consider them a call to perseverance. Endurance is a critical factor in any successful venture. Sudden success is so rare that it is almost nonexistent. Perseverance opens the heavy doors that lead to success in this life.

Most of us know the story of Christopher Columbus. On August 3, 1492, he sailed the "ocean blue" in search of a new land. He found that new land on October 12 after two and a half months of working, venturing, and sailing. Seventy-one days doesn't seem like all that long to an adventurer, but what we normally do not remember is that for ten years prior, from 1482 to 1492, he worked, asked, appealed and requested the funding for his passage to the New World. He would not have discovered our shores without the fortitude that led him to the

Spanish king and queen, Ferdinand and Isabella, who gave him the financial backing for the voyage. Columbus possessed the distinctive quality of perseverance.

On October 29, 1941, Winston Churchill, that grand old leader from England, revisited the Harrow School he had attended as a boy. That day he addressed the young men of Harrow with this challenge: "…never give in, never give in, never, never, never, never—in anything great or small, large or petty—never give in except to convictions of honor and good sense. Never yield to the force; never yield to the apparently overwhelming might of the enemy."[6] It was that kind of spirit which prevailed against Hitler and the German forces that came against our ally, England. Never, dear Christian, give up. Never, dear Christian, give in. Never, dear Christian, fall back. Always endure to the end!

NEVER GIVE IN

Every believer experiences suffering. Every person who follows Jesus has the calling of suffering applied to his or her life. We are destined to face the heat in life as Peter explains in 1 Peter 4. In verse 12 he tells us not to be surprised at the fiery ordeals. The word "fiery" is translated from the Greek word *puroo.* He continues by telling us not to be surprised at the "testing." That word comes from the Greek word *purosis.* Both of these words come from the root that gives us our word *pyromaniac.*

I reared a pyromaniac at my house, and if you have a son, you probably have a pyromaniac, too. There's just something about little boys that makes them fascinated by fire. (And if we are honest, their daddies are fascinated, too.)

When my son, Bennett, was young, we would go to the father/son RA campouts. Someone would bring a load of wood in the back of a pickup truck. If there were a hundred boys there, we would have a hundred campfires going. We would smoke up the whole north end of the county where we camped. Finally, the camp leaders had to make a rule that we could have only a certain number of fires in camp. The boys complained, but the moms had to deal with much less smoky-smelling laundry.

Bonfires and fireplaces are great, but when the fire of suffering comes, we don't like it, do we? But mark it down. The heat is coming if you stand for Jesus Christ. Suffering may come to your physical body. The heat may be applied in an intellectual challenge to your beliefs. The fire may be felt in your emotional makeup. The issue is not *if* suffering will arrive, because we are promised it will come. As a matter of fact, you cannot grow in spiritual maturity without it. Suffering is one of the essentials for developing Christian discipleship. We will either walk in His will and accept suffering or we will never reach the apex of God's presence He so yearns to bring about in our lives. So as we look closer at suffering, we will examine the four elements in the heat of the battle and our perseverance in the struggle.

THE SURENESS OF THE HEAT

First is what I call the sureness of the heat. First Peter 4:12 says,

> Do not be surprised at the fiery ordeal . . . as though some strange thing were happening to you.

Somehow we have come to the place today where we preach the gospel, ask someone to give his life to Christ, and then say, "Now your life is going to be the greatest life you've ever had." Indeed it will be; the longer I serve Him, the sweeter my life grows. But you share a bogus gospel if you promise people that upon becoming a Christian, all their troubles will be over. On the contrary, when you experience salvation, fiery trials are coming your way. It is not a strange or unique thing; it is common, widespread, and frequent. Peter continues in verse 14,

> If you are reviled for the name of Christ, you are blessed.

I could do without that blessing, couldn't you? Even so, if we are despised in the name of Jesus, we have been blessed. Therefore we should shout in gratefulness while we suffer. I know it's tough to do, but it is a matter of the will and the power of God within you to persevere all the way through the challenges you face.

THE HEAT IS SURE TO COME

In Colossians 1:24, notice what Paul has to say about the sureness of the heat.

> Now I rejoice in my sufferings for your sake, and in my flesh I do my share on behalf of His body (which is the church) in filling up that which is lacking in Christ's afflictions.

You may ask, "Does that mean Jesus' afflictions are not complete?" That is correct. Paul is not indicating that Christ's atonement is not satisfactory for salvation. Christ alone paid the cost for us all through His suffering and death on the cross. More accurately, Paul is explaining that the affliction of the cross did not end at the cross. Instead, the afflictions of Christ are passed on to us who are identified as part of His body, the church. Our suffering comes as we carry on the privilege of telling the gospel to the lost world. We can be joyful as we bear suffering in the name of Christ because we know that lives are changed and people will be saved.

Paul desired for us to understand that in our flesh we will share with His body (the church) in the afflictions for Christ's sake. We are to be vessels through which God, by our sufferings, completes us and carries on the work of the church. Until Christ returns, we, the body of Christ, will suffer just as Christ suffered here on earth. Recognize this, fellow believer: you will never come to maturity until you accept the call of suffering.

In 1988, Yellowstone National Park burned for eighty-one days and scorched 1.6 million acres. Nevertheless, by the year 2002, Yellowstone Park was never more lush and beautiful. Did we want it to burn? No. But even nature goes through the burning and scarring process. And when it happens, she bounces back with even greater brilliance. You, too, can pull through with great spiritual brilliance when you undergo suffering.

Be assured. Suffering is coming. You must decide before it arrives: (1) are you going to endure or (2) are you going to become acidic as wormwood—the plant known for its bitter and unpleasant taste? Unfortunately, that is what happens to most of us. When suffering comes, we get mad and/or we get even. We grow bitter and stay that way the rest of our lives.

WILL YOU ENDURE OR BECOME BITTER?

Why do we have unpleasant lay leaders in churches? Bitterness. A new pastor tries to change something simple, and some bitter deacon says, "Stop!" A new person shows up in class on Sunday morning and an unkind teacher filled with bitterness wants to know why he is here, where he came from—really gives him the third degree. The visitor thinks, *Huh? I just came in to ask if there's any coffee or doughnuts in the room.* Some people are so shriveled up with sourness that you cannot talk with them about anything. Christian, that is not the way you should respond to suffering. Learn this lesson—the sureness of suffering—and God will use it for His good.

THE SOURCE OF THE HEAT

After accepting the sureness of suffering that will come to us all, we determine the source of the suffering. Where does this suffering come from? What is the source of the heat? The source of the heat comes from at least four places: Satan, personal sin, the sin-cursed world, and spiritual devotion.

Satan is a source of the heat

The first place the heat can come from is Satan himself. In the book of Job, the Bible says the devil went after Job. Luke 13:11 tells the story of a lady whose back was all bent over. Her physical malady was from the devil. In Luke 13:16, Christ himself said that Satan had bound this lady for eighteen long years. Suffering can come from Satan. Not all of it does, but some of it can.

Personal sin is a source of the heat

Another source of our suffering is personal sin. We bring it on ourselves. First Peter 4:15 gives us a warning.

> By no means let any of you suffer as a murderer, or thief, or evildoer, or a troublesome meddler.

If you are a murderer, you are going to suffer for it. As a thief, you are going to suffer. An evildoer or even a troublesome meddler will suffer.

When we first moved to Pensacola, three young men broke into our home and stole everything they thought they could sell and all my children's videos to give to a girlfriend's child. Six weeks later, the police apprehended them and all our "stuff." The culprits had made a price list, but hadn't gotten around to selling the evidence of their crime. When we recovered our camera, we discovered they had taken pictures of themselves with my grandfather's shotgun and our electronics. (Brilliant crooks they were!)

I stood before the judge the day of their sentencing and told him I thought these boys should be sentenced to hear me preach every Sunday for the next three months. That would be punishment enough. The judge said he could not exactly do that, but looking down at those guys and pointing his long finger with unquestioned authority, said, "If you ever stand before me again, I will only have one question to ask you and that is whether or not you have heard Dr. Ted Traylor preach."

I personally invited all of them to church, but to my knowledge they never came, but as thieves, those young men brought on their own suffering. Being an evildoer will bring suffering. Being a busybody or an interfering person will bring suffering. There is truth in the scriptural caveat.

The sin-cursed world is a source of the heat

Satan does it. Your own sin can do it. Suffering also comes upon us from the sin-cursed world we live in. Even creation itself groans for a Redeemer. Earthquakes, fires, floods, hurricanes, and tsunamis all take lives and possessions, and we suffer. Famine and disease cause suffering. We suffer from natural disasters because this earth is no longer the Eden God created.

Why do innocent children suffer illnesses, starvation, and diseases? Why is it that some children have cancer and die at six months old? It is not because of the children's sin. It is not because of something they have done, or something their parents have done. God does not look down at the nursery and say, "I'm going to make this child mentally challenged," or "I'm going to make that child physically deficient." This suffering comes because we live in a world cursed by sin that indiscriminately attacks us and the people we love.

Why is the world racked with war and strife? Why are Americans sent to the battlefront today? Why must some die in war? They did not ask for it. Suffering can come simply because we are part of this imperfect and fallen world that will only know redemption when her Redeemer comes again.

Spiritual devotion to God is a source of the heat

Along with Satan, personal sin, and sin-drenched creation, suffering can take place because of our spiritual devotion to God. When we are spiritually dedicated unto the Lord God, we will answer the call to suffering and learn to endure through it. As Proverbs 17:3 says,

> The refining pot is for silver and the furnace for gold, but the Lord tests hearts.

The Lord will test us. That is certain. There are times when suffering comes to you straight from the hand of God. It is there to test us, to prove us, and to make us His obedient children.

When trials come from our spiritual devotion to God, the Lord will make it clear as to the source. There will be no guessing on your part—no, "I wonder if this test is from God." God-sent tests will bear witness to scriptural truth and lead to His ultimate glory when we persevere.

THE SURVIVAL OF THE HEAT

The sureness of suffering is coming. The sources of suffering appear from various places. Third, there is what I call the survival of the heat. How do you survive the heat in the midst of trials? Can you get through it? Can you make it? Peter states in 1 Peter 4:19,

> Therefore, let those also who suffer according to the will of God [one of the aforementioned sources of suffering] entrust their souls to a faithful Creator in doing what is right.

There are five steps for persevering through suffering. You may be asking yourself, "How in the world can I get through the suffering?" I want you to remember five things:

- **Remember your vision**
- **Revisit your goals**
- **Relax in the Lord**
- **Recommit to communion with God**
- **Rely on your friends**

With these five actions we can trust our Creator as we walk through the heat. He will always do what is right.

Remember your vision

To begin with, when you are suffering, remember your vision. What has God called you out to do? What has He led you to be? What is your God-given vision? Focus on that vision. You will persevere when you have God's vision for your life before you and you know you are in His will.

Revisit your goals

Next, I want you to revisit your goals. What goals are you trying to accomplish? Think about them. Write them down. Don't forget them. God may be using the pursuit of your goals to teach you endurance and perseverance. Those seemingly insurmountable obstacles in your path have divine purpose in your life. You may not be able to reach your goals any other way but straight through suffering.

Relax in the Lord

Third, relax in the Lord. Tension is a chief enemy of perseverance. When you allow tension to penetrate your life, you are less likely to stay in God's timing and direction. In Psalm 37, David challenged us to rest in our Sovereign God and wait for Him. That's easy to say, but hard to do, but we must if we want to persevere.

Recommit to communion with God

The greatest accomplishment of suffering is this: *it will drive you to your knees.* We have not fully learned how to pray. We have not fully learned to be in the Word. But we quickly realize that we cannot survive the heat without a personal daily walk with the Savior. Through suffering, we recommit to communion with God, our heavenly Father. He gives us strength to endure.

SUFFERING DRIVES US TO OUR KNEES

Rely on your friends

Finally—but not least of all—after you remember your vision, revisit your goals, relax in the Lord, and recommit to communion with God, then rely on your friends.

Your friends who have already endured suffering will now help you endure. God is faithful, He has His people everywhere, and they will assist you through your suffering. Rely on those friends.

Several years ago I went through the hardest time I have ever faced in my life as a pastor. I was ready to quit. I didn't want to quit preaching; I just wanted to quit my church. I didn't think I deserved the church, and I knew they didn't deserve me. I wanted out. I had been facing two very difficult circumstances.

One situation involved a racial issue that threatened the safety of my family. I had invited a local African-American preacher to speak at our church. He came and preached to our congregation. Soon after, I received an anonymous letter that read, "If you ever have another (expletive) preach in the pulpit, I'll burn your house down." I went home and informed Liz, "Honey, you're getting a new house." In spite of the danger, I decided not to allow this intimidation to determine my actions, and my godly deacons concurred. So I invited the African-American preacher back to my pulpit and had his entire choir come with him.

Worship that night was incredible. God was honored and the Holy Spirit's presence was evident. Some of the deacons escorted my family and me throughout the evening, and one of the deacons who was a deputy sheriff stayed at our home the entire time we were away. I relied on my friends and they came through for me.

Months later, we went through a difficult time in the release of a staff member. A group of people were unhappy with the change, and I received some surprising mail about it.

My wife was sent an unexpected letter addressed to "Jezebel." (If you find that humorous, you haven't studied 1 Kings lately.) The return address was one word— "Legion." That letter hurt, but revealed the source of the suffering.

During this troubling time, I was given unsolicited advice. I was told my time at the church was up, that I had probably done everything here I needed to do, and it would be best if I found somewhere else to go. If I could have found a place to move, I would have been gone in a minute. I was really down and wanted out. I didn't like my church and I didn't think they liked me. I knew I had not been pristine in everything I did involving the situation. I'm human just like everyone else, but I had tried to do what I felt was right and I was sick and tired of the whole mess. I just wanted out of there.

FRIENDS HELP YOU THROUGH THE SUFFERING

One night while Liz and Rachel were out together, Bennett and I went down to the mall to give away quarters (also known as "going to the arcade"). When my son and I returned home around 8:30 that night, three people were sitting on the curb by the mailbox in front of my house. I thought, *Well, this may be it—the firing committee has come.* I sent Bennett upstairs and I went outside.

I saw silhouettes of three men I knew and trusted. I walked down to the edge of the yard and asked, "What are you guys doing here?"

They said, "Well, Pastor, we've been on a little trip today."

"Where have you been?"

They replied, "You're always telling us about your home in North Alabama and that cool artesian water that runs out of the hills."

I nodded, slightly puzzled. "Yes?'

One of them spoke up and said, "Have you ever read 2 Samuel 23?"

"I've read the whole Bible, but refresh my memory on that chapter."

He said, "You remember when David was in the cave at Adullam?"

"Oh, yeah, over at Adullam and Rephaim. I've read the story."

My friend continued, "David was there fighting the Philistines, and he made this comment while hiding in that cave, 'Oh, I wish I had a drink of water from the well at Bethlehem.' That was David's hometown. Three of David's men broke through the lines, went down and drew water for the king to drink from the well at Bethlehem, brought it back in a gourd, and gave it to him. David told the Lord that because these men had risked their very lives for him, he would not drink the water. Instead, he poured it out as a libation to God."

Still unsure what this had to do with me, I said, "I remember."

Another of the men said, "Well, we rented a car at 5:30 this morning and drove 320 miles to your home. We sang hymns and prayed for you the whole way. When we got there, we drove to your house and asked your mother for a drink of water for our pastor."

As they handed me the quart-sized fruit jar of crystal-clear Pisgah, Alabama, water he said, "Pastor, we've brought you a drink of water from the well at your 'Bethlehem.'"

We then had what we call on Sand Mountain, a "Holy Ghost spell" right there in my front yard. We cried and shouted and prayed. These three precious men had driven almost 12 hours roundtrip to encourage me that day. I learned I could rely on my friends when I was walking through the fire.

Finally I said, “You guys better go on home.”

“Well, we have something else for you. You’ve told us that after God called you to preach when you were seventeen, there was a huge rock where you’d go and lie down to watch the Tennessee River running through the valley.”

“Yes,” I said, "it’s a beautiful place in Pisgah Gorge.”

“We asked your daddy to take us to that rock, and we took along a hammer and broke off two pieces and brought them back to you. Pastor, the same God who called you on these rocks will sustain you if you will stay with the One who is the solid rock of your soul.”

We had another spell that evening. Those two rocks are now outside my home office, and every now and then I stand on them and remember the faithfulness of God and the encouragement of those three men. When you are going through the fire, rely on your friends.

“Y’all better go home,” I said. “It’s nearly ten o’clock.”

“We have one more thing. Pastor, you know that rhododendron that grows up there? Well, we brought you some fresh flowers from home.”

They reached inside the car and brought out a two-pound Maxwell House coffee can. They had placed gravel in the bottom, filled it with water, and stuck a branch of rhododendron in it.

I said, “Boys, it’s a $50 fine to cut these flowers at the Pisgah Gorge.”

“We saw the signs, but we just had to bring them to you, and we heard a pastor once say it’s easier to get forgiveness than permission! So, if you will trust God, He will be the Lily of the Valley to your soul every day.”

Those flowers faded away but I took a picture of them and have that picture on my bookshelf at home. It reminds me that when I am going through the fire, I can rely on my friends.

Finally, they looked at me and one of them said, "Pastor, we've been talking about this. We want you to know something. We want you to know we will die for you."

"Now wait," I said.

"No. We have chosen our words carefully. We will lay down our lives for you. We believe you are God's man for our church, and we're here until the end. If you will remain biblically pure and faithful to your wife, we will lay down our lives for you."

When you are going through the fire, trust your friends. When you are going through the fire, be a friend. When you see others going through the fire, go get them a drink of water from the well at their Bethlehem.

Since that night, I have preached a sermon built around that illustration hundreds of times. I have seen scores of preachers encouraged. Ministries have been rekindled and relationships mended. Was it anything I did? No. It's not about me. It is about three men who ministered to me and helped me survive the heat.

If you ask, "Who are those guys?" I can't tell you. Sorry. In 2 Samuel 23, David's friends are unnamed. My friends and I have a bond. We will never tell who they are until they die. The names have been erased to protect the blessed! (I am also taking that as God's promise that I will outlive all of them, so I am not going to worry about entering eternity until after I have preached the second funeral.)

Will you be a friend to someone going through the fire? Will you hang on in the heat? You will survive if you learn to rely on the people God sends into your life.

THE SOVEREIGNTY OF THE HEAT

Finally, I want to show you what I call the sovereignty of the heat. Why do we go through suffering? The answer is found in 1 Peter 4:13.

> But to the degree that you share the sufferings of Christ, keep on rejoicing; so that also at the revelation of His glory, you may rejoice with exultation.

We suffer for the revelation of His glory. When we suffer and persevere, He reveals His glory in us and through us so that we may rejoice with delight. Then we can say, "Hallelujah! Glory to God!"

The only way for that to happen is for us to learn to keep pressing on. Persevere with hope and cheer while staying under the load. Perseverance is patiently enduring. We find the actual background of this word in the word *metamorphosis.*

The Cecropia moth is the largest silkworm moth in North America. When the Cecropia becomes an adult, it has an incredible wingspan of six inches or more. When the moth prepares to die, she finds a leaf and lays an egg. At the right time of year, that egg produces a fuzzy caterpillar that works its way through life eating leaves. At the time of its appointed death, the caterpillar will lie upon a leaf and emit a fiber of silk to wrap itself up very tightly until it makes a cocoon. After a certain period of time, it begins its metamorphosis.

> SUFFERING REVEALS GOD'S GLORY

Through God's divine design, that ugly worm becomes an extravagant moth. It begins kicking, gets its head out of the cocoon, then a wing breaks through. As it continues its struggle to emerge from its cocoon, the moth is fragile and wet. At this point, consider what could happen. Someone could come by, see the delicate moth struggle for release, and want to be of assistance. The person reaches over and helps the moth out of the suffering that nature intended to use for its glory. Sadly, that person has ruined the moth's life, for it is in the struggle for freedom that the blood is forced into the farthest extremities causing the wings to dry and lighten, enabling them to flutter so the moth can fly.

PERSEVERANCE IS PATIENTLY WAITING

You and I will never have a soaring faith until we persevere through our suffering. Without suffering we will never fly. We will never reach our full potential in God's kingdom. Every outstanding preacher, every excellent missionary, every great Christian you know—if they are honest with you—will confess they have had to walk through the fire. It is only in the fire that they are changed so they can wing to greater heights. For some, the suffering is a child who has gone astray. For some, it is a physical malady. For some, it is a struggle they have been through in the life of their church.

In 1895, James Chalmers, a missionary from the London Missionary Society, returned home to give a report about his difficult and dangerous work in New Guinea. At the conclusion of his report, he boldly stated that he was their missionary and he would go back to New Guinea to work with the savages even if it cost him his life. Chalmers returned and, indeed, the native cannibals killed him.

However, during World War II, the story is told that when soldiers came to the shores of this large island in the East Indies, there were no barbarous tribes. The gospel had changed the entire island. It was only through Chalmers' suffering that the glory of God was revealed. And it was only in his perseverance that the glory of God did the work.

Moses persevered through his struggles. For forty years he endured the wilderness, but he persevered.

Joseph was sold into slavery and later, based on a false accusation, was imprisoned by Potiphar for more than two years, yet he persevered.

Although Job lost his entire family, fortune, and health, he persevered through his suffering.

Most importantly, Jesus went to the cross and on that day on a hill far away when it became midnight at noonday—*Jesus persevered until his mission was finished.*

Will you persevere? Will you add perseverance to your faith, moral excellence, knowledge and self-control? If you persevere through your sufferings—no matter the cost—you will radiate His splendor and majesty. As you allow God's glory to come through your sufferings, He will transport you to the highest heights of His presence where you can experience a life full of indescribable joy. Persevere!

Several years ago, I shared my story about the three friends who ministered to me with a group of men from an association of country churches. I told them, "You need to go and love your preacher." Nothing much happened that night. After a time, my wife spoke about overcoming discouragement at a conference for ministers' wives. As an illustration, she also told about the three friends and the water. Afterwards, a young preacher's wife with tears rolling down her face came up to Liz and said she wanted me to know the rest of the story and its impact on their lives.

The young lady said they lived in a small house down a dirt road where traffic was rare. Her husband was pastor of a small, rural church with about 50 people in Sunday School. They were facing a period of real struggle and discouragement in their church.

Her husband and a couple of church members attended the associational meeting and heard me tell the "water story." The next evening she looked out the window and as far as she could see down the road were headlights of cars coming toward them. The cars began stopping at the house and men began getting out of the cars. The young wife said she thought, *Oh no. They've had a secret meeting at church and we're fired.*

Instead, the men knocked on the door and asked if they could come in. They crowded into that tiny living room. One man had a bucket he asked to fill with warm water. One man had a towel. Then they knelt before their pastor, took off his shoes and socks, and washed his feet. They declared to their pastor that they would forevermore serve as bondservants with him.

PERSEVERANCE BRINGS REWARD

The wife's countenance glowed as she asked Liz to tell me and those three men—whoever they are—what God had done through them. I emailed each with four words, "GOD DID IT AGAIN."

If you will persevere, heaven will record what God achieves through you. But if you shrink back, your wings may be crippled and you may never soar to the summits of God's grace. In Matthew 6:11, Jesus said that if you are reviled for Christ, you are blessed. So when the heat comes, shout, "Turn it up, Lord! Hallelujah! I'm ready to learn through suffering, but can I learn in a hurry?" We all want out of the heat, don't we?

We want the lush beauty without the fiery scars. But God's beauty shines forth the brightest through the scars left only after we have walked all the way through the heat of battle. Persevere and God will reveal His glory through you.

You may be a wife about to give up on your marriage. You want to quit. Let me encourage you to persevere and watch what God is going to do. Some of you may be ready to give up teaching. You are thinking, *I've taught for the last time. I'm going to give up and quit. Those people in my class don't appreciate me anyway.* Know this: being appreciated by those who listen is not a prerequisite for teaching.

You may be a person who is ready to quit church altogether. In your mind, you have already attended for the last time. Or, you used to sing in the choir, but you gave that up and started sitting about midway back in the congregation. Slowly you moved to the back pew, then to the balcony, and now you rarely come to church at all. You are about to quit on God. Don't! God has not quit on you.

OUR FIFTH NOTE IS THE CALLING OF SUFFERING

Those who are faithful to the end will be rewarded.

Paul told Timothy that if we endure in living out our Christian walk to the end, "…we shall also reign with Him" (2 Timothy 2:22). Persevere!

Can Christ count on you to walk in endurance? God wants to use you, as together we continue to "share the sufferings" of the Lord Jesus Christ. Persevere!

REPEAT

1. List the first five callings of God and beside each list the quality it develops.

   The call to…
   ______________________________, which is the call to______________________________

   The call to…
   ______________________________, which is the call to_____________________________

   The call to…
   ______________________________, which is the call to_____________________________

   The call to…
   ______________________________, which is the call to_____________________________

   The call to…
   ______________________________, which is the call to ______________________________

2. The next three callings are:
   ________________________,
   ___________________ ______________________, and
   ________________________.

3. What are the four elements in the fire of suffering?

4. What are four sources of suffering?

5. What are five steps for surviving suffering?

INTERPRET

6. What part can friends play as you go through the fires of suffering?

7. What is the difference between suffering for Jesus' sake and suffering for other reasons?

8. Who has been a trusted friend to you when you were enduring pain? How did that friend bless you?

9. Has there been a metamorphosis, a dramatic change, in your Christian growth as a result of suffering? Describe what happened.

PRACTICE

10. Do you know someone who is going through the fires of suffering? What do you plan to do to encourage that person?

11. Is there a pastor, church leader, or teacher who needs an encouraging word or your support? How do you plan to express this support?

PAUSE

Father, thank You for Your word of encouragement that I can make it through my sufferings. I pray, O God, that You will not only encourage me, but that You will also let me be a friend who encourages others to remain faithful as they go through the flame. For the suffering I have brought on myself by wrongdoing, I repent. Whatever comes, grant me endurance. Help me persevere. For Jesus' sake I pray. Amen.

6
The Calling of *Submission*

Recently I was reminded of a young husband who came to church, became a believer, and God changed his life. He decided he was going to overcome his selfishness and help his wife around the house. When he returned home, he decided to do all the laundry for one weekend. He reached in the laundry hamper, took out a shirt, held it up, then looked at the dials on the washing machine. He called to his wife, "What kind of water do you use? Hot, warm, or cold?" She called back, "Well, it's according to what it says on the label." He replied, "University of Alabama. Now what do I do with it?"

Some of us just have to work harder at being overcomers than others, don't we? In 2 Peter 1:5-7, Peter talks about being an overcomer when great trials come. He said if we are going to prosper in our Christian journey, we must begin with

FAITH, and you are to add
MORAL EXCELLENCE, to your moral excellence add
KNOWLEDGE, to your knowledge add
SELF-CONTROL, to your self-control add
PERSEVERANCE, to your perseverance add
GODLINESS, to your godliness add
BROTHERLY KINDNESS, and to your brotherly kindness add
LOVE.

With those eight words, like eight notes in an octave, we can reach spiritual maturity and come together to sing the songs of Zion. God's orchestration is complete when we begin with faith and include all these attributes in our lives.

To the fifth attribute, perseverance, we are to add the sixth—godliness. To learn about godliness, we read Paul's admonition to a young preacher in 1 Timothy 4:7-16.

> But have nothing to do with worldly fables fit only for old women. On the other hand, discipline yourself for the purpose of godliness; for bodily discipline is only of little profit, but godliness is profitable for all things, since it holds promise for the present life and also for the life to come. It is a trustworthy statement deserving full acceptance. For it is for this we labor and strive, because we have fixed our hope on the living God, who is the Savior of all men, especially of believers. Prescribe and teach these things. Let no one look down on your youthfulness, but rather in speech, conduct, love, faith and purity, show yourself an example of those who believe. Until I come, give attention to the public reading of Scripture, to exhortation and teaching. Do not neglect the spiritual gift within you, which was bestowed upon you through prophetic utterance with the laying on of hands by the presbytery. Take pains with these things; be absorbed in them, so that your progress may be evident to all. Pay close attention to yourself and to your teaching; persevere in

SUBMISSION IS THE CALL OF GODLINESS

> these things; for as you do this you will insure salvation both for yourself and for those who hear you.

The word *godliness* is actually two words put together. *Godliness* in the Greek New Testament is the word *eusebeia.* The front end, *eu,* means good, and *sebeia* means worship or devotion. Together the word means good worship. It is similar to our word *eulogy*. Once again, *eu* on the front of the word means good; *logos* on the end means word. When a person dies, someone gives a eulogy and says a good word about the person. In this scriptural context, godliness means good worship. It is devotion. It is submission. This godliness is found only in our bowing before the Lord God. Jesus said it this way in Matthew 22:37-38,

GODLINESS MEANS GOOD WORSHIP

> You shall love the Lord your God with all your heart, and with all your soul, and with all your mind. This is the great and foremost commandment.

I once heard a story about a great military leader, the Duke of Wellington. Two centuries ago he attended a small rural church in England. The church members were thrilled that the Duke of Wellington had come. They invited him to sit on the very front pew. It was their custom when taking the Lord's Supper for worshipers to come and kneel at the altar. From the communion table the clergy would offer the wafer and the wine to each partaker. As the duke went to kneel, an old beggar came and knelt alongside him. A man from the church came forward to rebuke the old man and said, "Sir, please move. Do you know who this is?" But the duke put out his hand and said, "Sir, stay right where you are. There are no dukes at God's altar."

When we come before the Lord God, we all come on level ground. We cannot come thinking we are someone special or a person of privilege. We come with the understanding that we are nothing without Him. That is where godliness is birthed. We bow before the Master because godliness demands submission. You must bow before the Lord with all your heart, with all your soul, and with all your mind. You will never know true worship until you answer the calling of submission.

Let's look at what it means to answer the call of submission, which yields godliness in your life and mine. I believe these eight attributes named by Peter are in a particular order. They are placed there by the breath of God and by the inerrant Word of God. Godliness follows perseverance. Submission follows suffering. And it is often out of suffering that we experience brokenness. We learn to bow our lives and come to the place where godliness can be developed within us. How do we get achieve godliness?

THE FOUNDATION OF GODLINESS

The foundation of godliness can be discovered when we understand what I call the backside, the underside, and the bottom of this word *eusebeia.* Three different insights combine to establish godliness in our lives. I want to examine each one separately.

Godliness is found in humility

The most obvious example of godly submission is humility. First Peter 5:6 says,

> Humble yourselves, therefore, under the mighty hand of God, that He may exalt you at the proper time.

The word *humility* in Latin comes from the word *humilis.* Out of that word we find the root word *humus.* Humus is the organic matter created when a plant or animal dies and decomposes. Eventually humus returns to the earth by becoming part of the soil, producing nourishment for plants and animals that are alive. That which is alive feeds off of that which has died. Literally, the death of plants and animals yields life to growing things.

GODLINESS REQUIRES HUMILITY

Where do we find life in the church? It is not in our self-exaltation. It is in our self-death and our humility. It is in submission to God as ruler of our lives. In John 3:30, John the Baptist said it well when he declared, *I must decrease and He must increase.* You see, the life of godliness is found in humility. The day we as Christians begin to think we are "something" on our own is the day we flounder in our pursuit of godliness. The day we believe we are too significant to bow at the altar is the day godliness ceases. The day any of us deems himself too important to do any job in the church, we have missed humility. We will never have the foundation for godliness.

I have watched deacon ordination ruin too many men. These men are seen serving the Lord, and are nominated, elected and ordained as deacons. Once they have a position or title, they think they have become "somebody." They do not understand that the New Testament meaning of the word *deacon* is servant. The first deacons served tables (Acts 6:2-3). I warn potential deacons that there is nobody lower in the church than a deacon, except the pastor.

You see, it is the humus, the *humilis,* the humility that enriches spiritual growth. It is the brokenness, the "bendability" of your life that yields godliness. Yet knowing this, some will say, "I'm just too scared of what people will think if I walk down the aisle and kneel and give my heart and life to Christ." If you are more concerned about what people think than what God thinks, you will never be a godly man or woman. Godliness comes from humility, and that spiritual nourishment emanates to everyone else who is trying to live for God.

Godliness is found in the fear of God

The second insight found in this word *eusebeia* is the fear of God. Matthew 10:28 says,

> And do not fear those who kill the body, but are unable to kill the soul; but rather fear Him who is able to destroy both soul and body in hell.

Jesus said we need not fear those who can destroy our bodies. He declared our greatest fear needs to be for the One who can deal with us not only physically, but in the spiritual realm as well. Understand that God is the One we need to fear.

The fear of God is not the same kind of fear we have when we spot a state trooper. Have you noticed that no matter how fast you are going, you tap your brakes when you see a flashing light? Even if we weren't speeding then, we're afraid we've been caught. I've been known to hit my brakes again while I am sitting still at a stop sign. But I'm not referring to that kind of fear. Nor am I talking about the fear you have of someone who has been abusive to you, either verbally or physically. That is legitimate fear that causes us to be downright scared.

This definition of the word *fear* used in this passage is even more than reverential awe. There should be some trepidation on our part when we come to God in reverence. A fear factor warns, "He is in charge and I am not. Therefore, I fear Him and will do as He says." When we walk into the presence of almighty God in submission to Him, there should be a healthy anxiety, yet it is a fear full of comfort.

FEARING GOD IS A PART OF BEING GODLY

Godliness is found in worship

Godliness is birthed in the foundation of humility. Second, it is found in the proper fear of God. The third part of this word formulates into "worship." Add to your perseverance *eusebeia,* "good worship." This is praise unto the Father. Godliness comes when you give Him glory and honor, and worship is exalting God as we bow in submission.

Christians worship in many different ways. We even put labels on our services to define the style such as traditional, contemporary, or blended. A gentleman once asked me, "Dr. Traylor, do you have traditional or contemporary worship?" I responded, "Neither." Then I mustered up all the self-sufficiency and arrogance I could (and I can muster quite a bit) and said, "We have authentic worship." He looked at me and said, "What is that?" I said, "I don't know, but it is as good as the words you are using." Whatever the style, authenticity is key. Our worship must be genuine and real.

Sometimes we worship with a praise chorus born out of victory. Sometimes we worship with a hymn born out of faith. It may not happen the same way every time, but I know this: when Jesus is high and lifted up, and I bow before Him, He touches me and then I know I have worshiped.

Sometimes I worship at home alone. Every Saturday night I go through the entire Sunday service by myself. I take the printed worship guide and I sing every song. I pray every prayer. I imagine baptizing every person. I preach every sermon note and I just have church at my desk. I can visualize our members gathered for worship, but I can worship when no one else is there. I get one-on-one with God. He is lifted up; I am bowed down. You, too, should have a time for private worship in your life.

PRAISE AND PRAYER DEVELOP GODLINESS

We also look forward to coming together corporately for worship. You see, there must be a time when we praise and honor the Lord together. Our strength is found through a foundation based on godliness. That foundation of godliness is found in humility, fear of God, and worship.

The Eiffel Tower was built in the late 1800s. It is an architectural work of art, 984 feet high—1063 feet with the antenna. We remember the beautiful images of this magnificent structure captured during the worldwide millennium celebration on January 1, 2000. The Parisian masterpiece was lit up in an incredible display of fireworks. But the real masterpiece was located underneath the Eiffel Tower. This great structure is supported by four massive masonry blocks. Two of the masonry blocks, the western foot and the northern foot, are closest to the Seine River where the ground is softer. During construction, an 800-ton hydraulic jack was built into each one of those feet. The engineers were able to adjust the structure until the tower was exactly level. The Eiffel Tower now rests on a solid and secure foundation.

In order for your life to be on a godly foundation, you must worship the Lord with all your heart, all your soul, and all your mind. No one else can see what the true foundation of your life is based upon. You know whether your foundation is firm or whether you are just pretending to be something you are not. You know if you are displaying a façade, a false appearance for others to see while actually concealing your true self. Only you and God know what is in your heart.

If you are going to be a godly individual, your life must rest on humility. It must rest on the fear of God and on the worship of our Lord and Savior, Jesus Christ.

THE FORMATION OF GODLINESS

After placing your life on the foundation of godliness, there must be what I call the formation of godliness. The foundation is laid on humility, fear of God, and worship. Then how do we form a "tower" of godliness, so to speak? The formation of godliness requires what I call working out, looking up, and pressing on.

From the beginning of Paul's first letter to Timothy, he compels the young preacher to stay with the Word of God. He warns Timothy not to believe something is true just because someone says it is truth, but to stay true to the Scriptures he had been taught.

Now notice what Paul says in 1 Timothy 4:7.

> But have nothing to do with worldly fables fit only for old women. On the other hand, discipline yourself for the purpose of godliness.

Discipline is a great word. It comes from the Greek word *gumnazo*, from which we get our word *gymnasium*. Just as it takes time in an exercise program to be physically fit, it takes time in the spiritual gym to exercise your faith muscles. That is exactly what Paul is speaking about in this text when he says to discipline yourself. If you are not disciplined, you will never run for the prize (1 Corinthians 9:24). Discipline yourself for the purpose of godliness. Work out!

Work out with discipline

If you belong to the body of Christ, you will find yourself already in the "gym" working out with other believers. In fact, if you don't work out with other people, you probably won't work out at all. You'll sleep in and you'll make excuses. Most of us won't last long if we don't have someone to keep us accountable. That is why the church is so very important.

We have to work out to develop godliness. Our workout must include three key disciplines found in 1 Timothy 4:13-16.

- Reading the scripture
- Developing spiritual gifts
- Exercising self-control

Read the Scripture

The first discipline in our workout is Scripture reading. A godly man or woman believes everything written in the Bible. This is our guidebook. This is God's Word to us, and we stand upon it.

But not only must we believe the Bible is the Word of God, we must read the Bible with a regular, disciplined plan. We must have personal Bible study so that we can grow in godliness.

Paul emphasized the importance of Scripture in 1 Timothy 4:13.

> Until I come, give attention to the public reading of scripture, to exhortation, and teaching.

Be attentive to God's Word

Have you ever noticed that sometimes in church when we read the Word of God, people will fidget? When the preacher opens the Book, we should listen. If you are not going to pay attention any other time, at least pay attention at the public reading of Holy Scripture. Show respect toward God's holy Word.

While attending a football game in Alabama when I was twelve, an incident happened that I will never forget. I was standing up on the next to the top row of the bleachers with a buddy of mine. During the playing of the national anthem, we were giggling and punching each other.

All of a sudden something hit me in the back of the head. I turned around to see this guy who was a retired Marine who knew my daddy. He had taken his big old ring, turned it over, and hit me in the back of the head with it. *Clunk!* Ouch! In no uncertain words he said, "Boy, when they play that song and they raise that flag, you stand still, you sing, and you listen!" Since that day I have not moved a muscle during "The Star Spangled Banner." I put my hand over my heart, I have one eye looking at the flag and one eye looking over my left shoulder for that Marine.

We Americans had become very lax in our patriotism prior to September 11, 2001. During the singing of the national anthem at sporting events, kids would run around and people would talk and keep on walking. Frankly, I was tired of that happening. But since that day, we are being much more respectful toward our flag and our country. We need to show respect and attention to our national symbol.

How much more should we show respect for the Lord God, the Maker of us all, and for His Word? The Bible is alive, sharper than a two-edged sword according to Hebrews 4:12. Would we pay more attention if the pastor unsheathed a glistening broadsword and began walking up and down the aisles quoting verses? Perhaps, but it's time we disciplined ourselves to be attentive to the Word of God every time we hear the precious Word read out loud. Practice standing attentively and listen carefully. It is an act of submission that is important in the formation of godliness in our lives.

Receive the preaching of God's Word

Not only should we practice the discipline of reading the Word, we should also exhort one another through the Word. Exhortation is my spiritual gift, and that's why I'm so passionate about this word. *Exhortation* literally means to call alongside. In Greek it is the *paraklesis—para,* alongside of, and *klesis,* or the call. When you hear the Word of God, it calls you to stand alongside our Lord. That is why you need to be in church on Sundays and whenever else the church gathers for worship and Bible study. You need to be where the Word of God is expounded. It takes discipline, but it is part of the spiritual formation workout.

RESPONDING TO GOD'S WORD IS ESSENTIAL TO GODLINESS

Attend small group Bible study regularly

Through teaching and instruction we learn the doctrines of Scripture. We gain wisdom through the teaching and learning that occurs during a Bible study class.

Some people do not like to be part of a small group because they are afraid they may be called upon to pray or read aloud. Perhaps you were embarrassed or intimidated in a small group setting and maybe you are still fearful about it.

Let me encourage you to try a small group again, because in a small group you will study scripture and hear doctrine, and it is there that you will experience fellowship. It is there that you will use your spiritual gifts. Get into a small group so that the teaching, the doctrine, and the instruction of the Word of God can infiltrate your life. Unless you discipline yourself in this area, you will never grow in the formation of godliness.

Develop and Practice Your Spiritual Gift

A second key discipline in your spiritual workout is developing your spiritual gift (or gifts—you may have more than one). First Timothy 4:14 says,

> Do not neglect the spiritual gift within you, which was bestowed upon you through prophetic utterance with the laying on of hands by the presbytery.

Paul is instructing Timothy to recognize that if someone is saved, he has at least one spiritual gift. When Timothy was saved, the Spirit of God came to live inside him, and subjectively he understood his spiritual gift.

The awareness of his spiritual gift was not only subjective, it was also objective because a prophetic word was spoken. Your spiritual gift is usually obvious to others, and they will speak an objective prophetic word to you. That person will see the hand of God upon and within you.

Before I understood the call to preach, people would say to me, "Have you ever thought about preaching?" And I would say, "Absolutely not. Not going to. Don't want to." Yet people continued to say they thought I ought to be a preacher—that God was going to call me to preach. There was that objective word from others coming to me. I finally had to submit.

Not only was it subjective and objective, but there was also a corporate word—the laying on of hands of the presbytery, the leaders of the church. My ordination was the recognition by the church of my giftedness. This is one reason why joining the church is so important. The body life of the church is essential. Some of you attend week after week, but never submit yourselves to the local church by membership. You need to surrender yourself and join a group of believers. If it calls for baptism, be baptized. If it calls for repentance, repent. Whatever it takes, subject yourself to membership at the local church.

> GODLINESS INCLUDES USING YOUR SPIRITUAL GIFT

The corporate influence of the local church brings accountability to your life. There is a stirring of your spiritual gifts that you will encounter no other place. It is important to join the church.

I called a lady recently to say we were glad she visited our church. She said to me, "Thank you." Then with embarrassment, she sheepishly said, "I've been visiting for five years. I finally filled out a visitor's card."

"Five years? Well, you have four to go before you set the record." (A couple once confessed they visited for nine years before joining.)

We laughed a little and she admitted, "I know I need to join the church."

So being the kind, compassionate person that I am, I said, "Well, why don't you? Don't tell me you need to. Just do it." She did.

The body life of the church makes a difference in your life and in your world. You do not need to be a lone ranger sitting on the creek bank. When a person tells me he worships in nature, I'm fairly certain his offering goes for bait! You don't need to spend God's money on fish food. You need to be a part of the local church. It is a discipline that will yield godliness in your life.

Develop and Exercise Self-control

Added to the discipline of reading Scripture and developing spiritual gifts in your life is the third key discipline in our workout—exercising self-control. We will never have godly self-control in our lives unless we answer God's calling to submission. First Timothy 4:16 says,

> Pay close attention to yourself and to your teaching; persevere in these things; for as you do this you will insure salvation both for yourself and for those who hear you.

Pay close attention to yourself. Watch. Evaluate. Look at your life. Reread chapter 4 in this book. Have you developed self-control? Ask yourself, "Am I the same person I have always been?" If you are, then ask, "God, what is it that I am not doing now that would help me to move toward more self-control? Teach me to increase and apply this discipline to my life in days to come."

The formation of godliness in the believer's life requires a regular workout in the areas of Scripture, spiritual gifts, and self-control. Join God's "gym" and work out with discipline.

Look up and fix your hope on God

The formation of godliness also requires us to learn to look up. In 1 Timothy 4:10, Paul writes,

> For it is for this we labor and strive, because we have fixed our hope on the living God, who is the Savior of all men, especially of believers.

Why should you fix your hope on God? Paul points out two reasons. Foremost, Christ is the Savior of all men. What does that mean? Some people today teach that through universalism, everyone is going to heaven regardless of whether one believes in the atonement of Jesus or not. This is false doctrine. According to the Word of God in Matthew 7:13, Jesus said there is a narrow way to heaven, and few find it. There is also a broad way that, sadly, many more will find. Those who travel the broad way are going to hell. Those who travel the narrow way of Christ are the only ones going to heaven. Jesus never taught a universal salvation. Jesus declared Himself "the way" in John 14:6.

Jesus is the Savior of all men. But what does that mean? It means there is a common grace for all mankind. You see, God loves every person. Some people propose that Jesus did not die for the sin of everyone, but only for those who are going to be saved. This text says He is the Savior of *all men.* He offers a common grace. God loves every man, woman and child, whether each person is going to believe in Him or not. It means that Jesus came with every soul in mind.

THERE IS A COMMON GRACE

As Jesus walked here on earth preaching the gospel, He continually implored all people to come if they would believe. There was a common and broad spreading of the seed of the gospel and sharing of the grace of God. Fix your hope on Him because of common grace, and fix your hope on Him because of saving grace. Christ is the Savior of all men. The believer must place his faith in the Lord Jesus Christ and trust Him. Therefore, not only common grace, but also saving grace has come into our lives.

Do you have your eyes fixed on Him? You cannot trust anything else to get you to heaven except Jesus and Jesus alone. You have to focus your eyes on Him. Many of you have your focal point on something else.

Some of you have your eyes set on elephants, gators, and tigers (of the sports team nature). Some of you have your gaze locked on checking accounts, stocks, and bonds. Others have your eyes directed on your families, your children, or your grandkids. None of these things is inherently evil or detrimental to the formation of godliness unless it takes your gaze off the cross. Fix your eyes on Jesus. *Look up!*

Have you ever noticed that we tend to look upward only when trouble comes—whether it is in our finances, with our family, or as a fan? If our team is losing, we start praying. If the stock market drops, then we begin looking to God. If our family suffers, then we hit the altar in a panic. That's because these things are our focus instead of the Lord. When we fix our eyes on Jesus and live with the calling of submission on our lives, we trust the Lord with all these things every day. We can enjoy the journey, live our lives with our families, make a contented living, and give abundantly of all we have, but do it with God's summons to fix our gazes on Him. *Look up!*

Press on when the pain comes

Work out, look up, and then press on. Paul tells us in 1 Timothy 4:15 to,

> Take pains with these things; be absorbed in them, so that your progress may be evident to all.

Godliness has a cost. A few years ago a television commercial touted a battery-powered device that would tone your abs simply by strapping it to your waist and turning it on. I wanted to say to the guy selling the gizmo, "Let me get this straight. If I buy this equipment and wrap it around my middle, my two-liter will become a six-pack? No kidding?"

Of course not! Face it. My muscles aren't going to become sculpted without hard work, pain and strain. That's why I have soft abs. I haven't taken any pains to improve their muscle tone. No sit-ups. No running. No workout. I admit I quit.

I am amazed at guys who can bench press 300 pounds or more. But when I watch them train, sweat, grit their teeth, and push themselves to lift pound after pound, I realize it's not amazing—it's hard work. They press on at the bench press.

In basketball games, our coach would sometimes call for a full-court press. We all went after the other team, guarding each player for the whole length of the court. We pressured them to force a turnover and get the ball. It was hard work. We had to submit to the coach and each other and couldn't stop even though our lungs were burning. If one player quit, the press wasn't effective, so we had to press on when the pain came.

Friend, if you are going to be godly, you have to press on. You will have to absorb some things that hurt. You will have to give up some things in submission to God. There is no easy way, no pill to swallow, no twelve-step plan that you can sign up for to help you trust God. You must press on with Him. No pain, no gain. That is what a personal trainer will tell you in the weight room. That is what I am telling you must happen in God's "gymnasium" if you wish to succeed in the formation of godliness in your life. *Press on!*

THE FRUIT OF GODLINESS

After establishing a foundation of godliness and then working through the formation of godliness in your life, visible fruit will be produced. People around you will see at least three characteristics clearly.

Godliness Yields Confidence

The first thing that godliness will yield is confidence. In 1 Timothy 4:12, Paul gives Timothy further instruction. (And if you are a teenager, you need to know this verse.)

> Let no one look down on your youthfulness, but rather in speech, conduct, love, faith and purity, show yourself an example of those who believe.

He reminds Timothy that youthfulness is not a hindrance to godliness. Just because he is young does not mean Timothy cannot be confident in his spiritual life. Paul then challenges him to be an example of a man whose life is lived in submission to God.

I imagine that sounded rather daunting to a youthful preacher. I remember being the new pastor and younger than all my deacons. I had to take this verse to heart and be confident. But whether you are young or old chronologically or spiritually, confidence in Christ comes from practice. We have to practice the disciplines of God to grow in our maturity in Christ.

A basketball player can successfully complete the winning free throw at the end of a game because he has thrown a million during practices. He's been working out and practicing hard, and that brings out his confidence. When there is a technical foul called by the referee and the game is tied, the coach is looking for the player with the best free throw shooting percentage who he knows has the confidence to make the play. That player will walk over to the referee and reach for the basketball as if to say, "Give me that ball, I'm ready."

When I played basketball in junior college, I could hit a free throw with my eyes shut (perhaps a slight exaggeration). I had learned the fundamentals in high school from Coach Cooley. He made us hit ten free throws in a row before we could leave practice. I had confidence! The guys without confidence were over there hiding behind the guy at the end of the bench thinking, *Lord, let him choose somebody else.* But confidence will cause you to say, "Give me that ball. I want to shoot it. I've done my practice work."

THERE IS A CONFIDENCE IN GODLINESS

All of us need to develop confidence in our Christian lives. We do that by establishing a strong foundation of godliness and practicing the disciplines that bring about the formation of godliness in each of us. It takes dedication, discipline, and submission.

Teenagers, if you want to have confidence in living for God, practice and press on. Don't let anybody look down on your faith. Don't let an unbeliever look down on your faith. When you go off to college, don't let an infidel in a biology class look down on your faith. The first thing godliness gives you is confidence. You can say, "I am with God; He is with me, and we will walk together." Stand with God. Stand up, stand out, speak up, and speak out for Christ. Godliness brings confidence.

Godliness Yields Character

Not only does godliness yield confidence, but it also yields character. In 1 Timothy 4:12, Paul shows us that character will produce godliness in five areas: in your speech—what you say; in your conduct—what you do; in your love—what you are passionate about; in your faith—what you believe; and in your purity—how you live.

What does your speech say about your character? According to James 3:8, "No one can tame the tongue; it is a restless evil and full of deadly poison." Have you submitted your tongue to the lordship of Jesus Christ? A godly heart produces godly speech.

I remember singing a song in the primary department that said, "Oh, be careful little eyes what you see…be careful little feet where you go." That is conduct in a nutshell. What you do speaks more loudly than what you say. What does your conduct say about your character?

Your character is revealed in what you love with all your heart. Godly people love Jesus more than anything in their lives. Then they can love everyone else and everything else in the proper perspective. What are you passionate about?

Do you live what you say you believe? Galatians 2:20 says, "The life which I now live in the flesh, I live by faith in the Son of God." Living a life of faith in God produces godliness, and godliness in your life yields the fruit of character.

A person with a godly character will live a life of purity. To live in purity, we must remove everything unholy from our lives that separates us from God. The godly teen will take the True Love Waits challenge and keep it. The man with a godly character will not knowingly cheat on his taxes. The godly woman will not be a demanding diva. You get the picture.

Godliness Yields Submission

A person living with Christian confidence and character will be a person living in submission—the calling of godliness. That person has made himself a bondservant of the Lord Jesus Christ.

Each person who joins our church is given a towel. It is the size of a normal hand towel, but it has a special design and purpose. On the towel is printed the word *bondservant.* Why do we give a towel? The example Jesus shows us in John 13 illustrates what we should do to minister to our fellow believers. Jesus took off His outer garment, took a towel, bent down, and washed the disciples' feet.

Not long ago I had lunch with a Freewill Baptist. I asked him, "What's the difference in a Southern Baptist and a Freewill Baptist?"

He said, "Well, some Freewill Baptists don't believe in the eternal security of the believer. But I do."

"So do we."

Then he said, "The only other difference in a Southern Baptist and a Freewill Baptist is that we have three ordinances instead of two."

"You do?"

"Yes, sir. We do baptism by immersion. We have the Lord's Supper."

"Yes, and the third is…?" (I knew what was coming.)

"We practice washing feet."

"Describe how you do that" I asked.

"At the end of a service we send all the men into one room and all the ladies into another room. They all have a basin."

I asked, "Do they take off their own shoes?"

"Most of the time. We take our shoes off and wash each other's feet. We tell each other we love them, and then we all congregate back together and sing a hymn and go out."

Do you know how humble you must be to wash another person's feet? Sure, you can wash feet as a routine and be hardhearted. You can be baptized and be hardhearted. Only God and you really know what is in your heart, but that is where godliness must begin—in your heart. It is the call to the discipline of submission.

THE CALL TO GODLINESS IS OUR SIXTH NOTE

You must diligently and daily work out in God's gym. Endure the pain of exercising your faith and suppressing your ungodly desires. Strengthen your practice of worship and the disciplines of godliness. Develop the self-control and willingness of the bondservant. Be a person of godliness who lives in confidence, character, and the calling of submission to the Lord Jesus Christ.

REPEAT

1. Fill in these six callings of God.

   ____
   which is the call to salvation

   ____________ ________________
   which is the call to separation

   ____
   which is the call to sanctification

   ____
   which is the call to service

   ____
   which is the call to suffering

   ____
   which is the call to submission

2. The next two callings of God are ____________
   _____________ and ____________________.

3. What two Greek words are put together to form the word *godliness*, and what does each mean?

   ____
   which means ____________________, and
   ____
   which means ________________________.

4. Based on the meanings for these Greek words, our word godliness means ___________ ________________.

5. What three ideas form the foundation of godliness?

6. What three disciplines are included in a believer's workout?

INTERPRET

7. What is the relationship between discipline and submission?

8. How does *humus* relate to submission?

9. Why is it important to be a member of a local church?

10. What does attending small group Bible study contribute to your spiritual development?

PRACTICE

11. How do you intend to be more receptive to the Word of God?

12. If you are not a member of a local church and/or a small group Bible study, what do you intend to do about it? When and how do you intend to do this?

13. What response will you make to someone who belittles your faith and/or worship practices?

PAUSE

Father, I ask that You grant me godliness in my life. Show me the words and ways that honor and praise You. Help me see the holiness in You that it may create a reverent fear and humility in my soul. Thank You for Your Word that I am privileged to read and hear and study with fellow believers. I bow my head and heart in submission to You. Thy will be done in all things, Lord. In Your holy name I pray.
Amen.

7
The Calling of *Sharing*

We have reached the seventh note of the octave in the eight callings of God. We are coming closer to composing and rejoicing in a full melody. Each chapter of this book has introduced one of the callings found in 2 Peter 1:5-7, which tells us to begin with

FAITH you are to add
MORAL EXCELLENCE, to your moral excellence add
KNOWLEDGE, to your knowledge add
SELF-CONTROL, to your self-control add
PERSEVERANCE, to your perseverance add
GODLINESS, to your godliness add
BROTHERLY KINDNESS, and to your brotherly kindness add
LOVE.

In Hebrews 13:1-6, we read about what Peter calls brotherly kindness and what I refer to as the calling of sharing. After accepting the calling of godliness, we must learn to apply brotherly kindness to our lives. Our word *philadelphia* comes from this Greek phrase. Hence, Philadelphia, Pennsylvania, is the city of brotherly love.

BROTHERLY KINDNESS CALLS US TO SHARE

The front half of *philadelphia* is the word *philos*, which means love—the kind of love between friends. *Adelphos,* which means brother, forms the last half of this word. So it is a brotherly friendship or a brotherly kindness that causes us to love others and treat others as we would our brothers or sisters.

THE REVELATIONS FROM BROTHERLY KINDNESS

Brotherly kindness reveals at least three things. First, it reveals to the world our identity with Christ. John 13:35 says,

> By this all men will know that you are My disciples, if you have love for one another.

When brotherly kindness is evident in our lives, everyone will know we are followers of Jesus.

Brotherly kindness also reveals our true identity, not only to others, but also to ourselves. First John 3:14 says,

> We know that we have passed out of death into life, because we love the brethren. He who does not love abides in death.

If *philadelphia* is not apparent, we are not alive in our spirits. But we know we have eternal life and we are sure of our eternity with Jesus when brotherly kindness is a part of our daily walk.

Not only does this brotherly kindness reveal who we are to the world and who we are to ourselves, but brotherly kindness also reveals the Savior's pleasure in us. Psalm 133:1 says,

> Behold, how good and how pleasant it is for brothers to dwell together in unity!

For brothers to exist in unity, brotherly kindness must dwell with them. When we present a united front to the world in our families, homes, and churches, the world knows it is good, we know it is pleasant, and God is pleased.

The Word of God further explains *philadelphia* in Hebrews 13:1-6.

> Let love of the brethren continue. Do not neglect to show hospitality to strangers, for by this some have entertained angels without knowing it. Remember the prisoners, as though in prison with them, and those who are ill-treated, since you yourselves also are in the body. Let marriage be held in honor among all, and let the marriage bed be undefiled; for fornicators and adulterers God will judge. Let your character be free from the love of money, being content with what you have; for He Himself has said, "I will never desert you, nor will I ever forsake you," so that we confidently say, "The Lord is my helper, I will not be afraid. What shall man do to me?"

After World War II, a wall was built in the German capital that separated East Berlin from West Berlin. During the Cold War, friends were separated from friends. Brothers were separated from brothers. In 1987, while visiting West Berlin, President Ronald Reagan delivered that memorable request at the Bradenburg Gate at the Berlin Wall where he implored the General Secretary of the Soviet Union, "Mr. Gorbachev, tear down this wall!" In 1989, the wall came down.

I heard a story about an incident that happened while the wall was very much a part of the citizens' lives. One Christmas the people on the East German side filled sacks with trash. They tied them with bows and threw them over the wall and yelled, "Merry Christmas!" Those who found the sacks in West Berlin took them and filled them with gifts, toys and fruit instead. They retied the ribbons and threw them back over the wall with a note attached: "Let each give what each has."

I don't know if that story is true, but if you are a believer in Christ, give what you have—Jesus in you. You do not give wrong for wrong. You do not give offense for offense. You give *philadelphia*—brotherly kindness, the love of Jesus within you.

We need to give it out in abundance. Why? Because the world takes much of its notion of God from those of us who say we belong to his family. The world will "read" us more than they will ever read the Bible. Your neighbors are "reading" you, your coworkers are "reading" your attitude. Your family members are "reading" your expressions of brotherly kindness. What does the book of your life reveal about you?

Read Hebrews 13:1 again.

> Let the love of the brethren continue.

Philadelphia is to continue on and on. This is not *agape* love which is God's kind of love, but rather a friendship kind of love. Where do we show brotherly kindness. How do we share this brotherly friendship to others? In these first six verses of chapter 13, the writer of Hebrews outlines three areas. We are to continually show brotherly kindness through ministry, in marriage, and with our money.

THE CONTINUITY OF BROTHERLY KINDNESS THROUGH MINISTRY

Brotherly kindness is manifested on a continual basis through ministry to the people around us. Opportunities abound. We must be aware of the people God sends across our paths. Each one affords a chance to share His love through ministry. Hebrews 13:2-3 gives two specific groups of people to whom we must continue showing brotherly kindness—strangers and those who suffer.

LOVE IS EXPRESSED IN HELPING OTHERS

Show brotherly kindness in ministry to strangers

The first place you show your brotherly kindness is through ministry to strangers. Notice verse 2.

> Do not neglect to show hospitality to strangers, for by this some have entertained angels without knowing it.

That word *hospitality* has the same root as *philadelphia. Philos* is the root word of friendship. Do not neglect to show this friendship or hospitality to people you have never met, people you do not even know. This is the ministry to strangers.

When you look up *stranger* in a thesaurus, you'll find entries like outsider, visitor, new arrival, foreigner, unfamiliar person, and "new kid in town." Those terms make us uncomfortable when they should make us empathetic. We've all been a stranger at one time or the other. We don't mind showing brotherly kindness to people we know, but we must go out of comfort zones if we are to obey the Word of God. Through ministry to strangers, some of us have unsuspectingly been in the company of angels.

That is exactly what happened to Abraham in Genesis 18. When three strangers came by, Abraham ministered to them. After spending a little time with them, he suddenly understood that they were angels of God. It also happened to Gideon in Judges 6. After a lengthy encounter, Gideon realized he was with the angel of the Lord. It happened to Manoah, the father of Samson, the Nazirite in Judges 13. Without knowing, both Manoah and his wife were visited by the angel of the Lord concerning the birth and upbringing of their son, Samson. Only after the angel ascended from them in flames of fire did they comprehend who their visitor had been.

I am occasionally asked, "Have you ever entertained angels?" My answer is, "Yes, one time that I know about." I had been preaching in Gadsden, Alabama, and was returning home on I-65. I was traveling with my former youth pastor, Eddie Walker. I was sleeping and he was driving. Suddenly I felt the car slow down and then come to a stop on the side of the interstate. I looked at the clock. It was 12:02, just after midnight.

I said, "What are you doing?"

He replied, "We have to stop and help somebody."

"We're not stopping and helping anybody at this time of night."

"Just trust me, Pastor." When a youth minister says, "Just trust me" and it is 12:02 a.m., I am immediately cautious! I was still trying to wake up completely as he jumped out and ran back down the shoulder of the highway.

I looked in the rearview mirror and saw an eighteen-wheel truck parked on the side of the road, and Eddie was running toward it. A young man, whose name we learned later was Corky, had gone to sleep while driving, causing his car to leave the road and run up under that huge truck. Suddenly fire flickered underneath his car. Within moments I ran back to see if I could help. Those who had also stopped to help were trying to cut Corky out of the seatbelt that had him pinned in. We finally pulled him out through the window just before flames engulfed the car. The car and the truck were destroyed.

Things were chaotic. Eddie tried to stop Corky's bleeding while others futilely tried to use a fire extinguisher on the flames. Seemingly out of nowhere, a man was on the scene and began calmly applying first aid to Corky. He had a backpack and was busy taking out bandages and putting them on Corky's injuries. Things were still happening quickly as the paramedics arrived. Just a few moments later I looked at Eddie and asked, "Where's that doctor—the one with the backpack?"

He looked around and said, "I don't know, but let's find him."

We looked high and low, scanning the faces of the people all around. The stranger was gone as if he vanished into the night air. We never saw that man again. Was he an angel? I don't know, but he was angelic to me, and I can guarantee he was angelic to Corky.

I still don't know for sure what happened that night. We were thrust into that scene the moment Eddie stopped to help. I do know that months later, Eddie led Corky to faith in Christ. Several years ago some of our church members met him when he visited our church. As we met again, Corky hugged me and thanked me for stopping and saving his life, but he was even more grateful for the gospel that had saved his soul.

Do not neglect to show hospitality to strangers. You never know as you get involved in ministry when angels may come upon the scene.

Show brotherly kindness in ministry to the suffering

Not only is there a time for ministry to strangers, but there is also a time for ministry to the suffering. Notice what the Scripture says in Hebrews 13:3,

> Remember the prisoners, as though in prison with them, and those who are ill-treated, since you yourselves also are in the body.

The writer is referring here to those who have been imprisoned for preaching the gospel. These are people who have been mistreated and have been placed in prison for the wrong reason—simply for obeying God.

Today, whether a person is falsely incarcerated or is guilty of every crime of which he was accused, we must minister to prisoners through their suffering. Many others who suffer are ill and hospitalized. There are those who are brokenhearted from the experience of divorce. Victims of tragedy and pain are all around us, and we must be faithful to minister to them as well.

Jesus said in Matthew 25:39-40,

> "And when did we see you sick, or in prison, and come to you?" and the King will answer and say to them, "Truly I say to you, to the extent that you did it to one of these brothers of Mine, even the least of them, you did it to Me."

When we visit those who are in prison, it is as if we were visiting Christ Himself. And if we do not visit, it is as if we do not care for Christ. The greatest testimony we have as Christians is when we get our hands dirty helping suffering people. When we hurt right along with those in brokenness, when we minister to the ill treated, when we are involved in touching their lives, we are ministering to Jesus.

HURTING AS OTHERS HURT IS BROTHERLY LOVE

You may say, "Well, I don't have anything to give." I believe everybody has something to give. You may say, "I don't know how much time I can spare." Do you have a willing heart? If you do, then just say, "Here I am, Lord. Use me." Make a visit, spend some time with the hurting, feed the hungry, intercede in prayer for the suffering. Brotherly kindness will flourish as you share in ministry. We as Christians and as churches must set our goal to show brotherly kindness to those in need.

THE EXPRESSION OF BROTHERLY KINDNESS IN MARRIAGE

A second area where brotherly kindness needs to continue is in our marriages. Hebrews 13:4 says,

> Let marriage be held in honor among all, and let the marriage bed be undefiled; for fornicators and adulterers God will judge.

If you are asking what in the world brotherly kindness has to do with marriage, then evidently you are not married. You see, your spouse must also be your friend, and there has to be a brotherly kindness toward your mate.

There are two things I want to say about this. We must have marriages of honorable bonds and honorable beds.

Let marriage have an honorable bond

First, we need to make marriage an honorable bond. How do we do this? We must always speak highly of marriage—the institution in general and your own marriage specifically. Husbands and wives should never say a negative word in public about marriage or their mates, even in a joking manner.

Place Christ as the head of your home. Bow before the Lord as a couple and as a family and dedicate your home to Him. You can pray something as simple as, "Christ, we are going to serve you above all." Then do it.

Fulfill your role in marriage. If you are the man at your house, be the head of your home. As the husband, you will be required to give an account one day for being the spiritual leader of your household, and whether or not your home counted for God. Christ declared that you, the husband and father, are to model His example in how He treats His bride, the church. You can abdicate your leadership, but you will stand in judgment for it. Let love and respect regulate your home.

The late Dr. E. V. Hill, former pastor of Mount Zion Baptist Church in Los Angeles, told this story. A man in their church was beating his wife. They sent the elders to him a first time, but the husband did it again. They sent the elders a second time, again admonishing him to stop abusing his wife. Unfortunately, the husband continued, so Dr. Hill sent the elders a third time. This time he instructed the elders to let the man know that if this abusive behavior continued, he would receive similar treatment. Dr. Hill said that following this third visit the man stopped abusing his wife.

While some men beat their wives, I've heard of some wives who are as mean as junkyard dogs. As a wife, honor and revere your husband. Be that loving helper he wants and needs. Say to him, "Well done." When I go home from church after preaching on Sunday morning, I find my wife and my lunch waiting for me. I can count on my right hand the number of times she did not say something like, "That was a great message today." (I know she has lied a few times.) She is building me up by saying, "Well done."

I have a pastor friend who lost his church and almost lost his family after an indiscretion. He later told me, "I've been married over fifteen years, and my wife has never said to me, 'I'm proud of you.'" May that be a clarion call to honor and respect your spouse. He or she should be your best friend in the world. We must continually display brotherly kindness in our marriages. Let marriage have an honorable bond.

> EXPRESS BROTHERLY KINDNESS, RESPECT, AND LOVE TO YOUR SPOUSE

Let marriage have an honorable bed

Second, the writer of Hebrews says not only to have an honorable bond, he also says let marriage have an honorable bed. Hebrews 13:4 says to let the marriage bed be undefiled. The word *undefiled* means unsoiled, not dirty, not corrupted or profaned. Get the picture? We are further told that,

> . . . fornicators and adulterers God will judge.

The word *fornication* is from the Greek word *porneia.* Our word *pornography* comes straight from that root word. Pornography is a killer of marriage whether it comes from the

Internet, television, movies or magazines. All Christians must guard their hearts against this addictive evil.

A word of warning here: if you want to keep your marriage free from adultery, there is a bunch of junk (for lack of a better word) you should not watch on television. Have you ever noticed that actors hop in and out of bed with anybody and everybody? No morals, no consequences, no conscience. Writers rarely have characters show concern for the heartache they will project on the people in their lives. We should all follow the example of one of the mothers in my church. She placed a sign on their television that reads, I WILL SET NO WORTHLESS THING BEFORE MY EYES (PSALM 101:3). We must heed David's words if the marriage bed is to remain undefiled.

Taking a vow to live forever with one person, and then going to bed with another, is like calling a terrorist and asking for a suicide bomb to explode in your life. Chapters 5 and 6 of Proverbs speak very directly with a stern warning against allowing lust to gain a foothold in our lives. Proverbs 7 warns emphatically about avoiding the harlot. Proverbs 6:22-25 says,

> When you walk about, [the commandments of God] will guide you; when you sleep, they will watch over you; and when you awake, they will talk to you. For the commandment is a lamp, and the teaching is a light; and reproofs for discipline are the way of life, to keep you from the evil woman, from the smooth tongue of the adulteress. Do not desire her beauty in your heart, nor let her catch you with her eyelids.

Recently I was downtown having lunch with one of the guys on our pastoral staff. After being seated we noticed a private business luncheon going on. I turned to my associate and said, "No wonder everybody is sleeping with everyone else's wife. Look around this room." There were women dressed like harlots on every side. They left some husband that morning, put on their makeup on the way to work with intentions to look good for the boss. When they left home, they had no long eyelashes to flutter or wonderful smell to savor. They entered the workplace dressed to entice, and their bosses are being led "…as an ox goes to the slaughter" (Proverbs 7:22). I told my fellow minister, "Whatever you do, don't let me out of your sight. You take care of me." Then I warned him, "You better not mess up either. I'm not very big but I'm wiry and I'll beat your eyes out!"

Adultery is deceptive and makes you dumb. "He does not know that it will cost him his life" (Proverbs 7:23). I've heard so many excuses. "My needs aren't being met." "I didn't think anyone would find out." "My wife doesn't understand me." "I deserve a little bit of happiness." You may think those are good reasons, but trying explaining away your sin to God.

Adultery will make you poor. Think hotel rendezvous reservations, secret cell phone lines, divorce lawyers, court fees, alimony, child support. And that is just the financial cost.

> For on account of a harlot one is reduced to a loaf of bread, and an adulteress hunts for the precious life. Can a man take fire in his bosom, and his clothes not be burned? [*NO.*] Or can a man walk on hot coals, and his feet not be scorched? [*NO.*] So is the one who goes in to his neighbor's wife; whoever

GO HOME AND LOVE YOUR MATE

> touches her will not go unpunished. Men do not despise a thief if he steals to satisfy himself when he is hungry; but when he is found, he must repay sevenfold; he must give all the substance of his house. The one who commits adultery with a woman is lacking sense. He who would destroy himself does it. Wounds and disgrace he will find, and his reproach will not be blotted out.
>
> Proverbs 6:26-33

Is adultery forgivable? Yes. But it brings a reproach you will never totally overcome. Your spouse will never fully trust you again. Dear man or woman, if you are already flirting with someone other than your spouse, come to your senses. Wake up! Repent! Go home and love your wife. Love your husband. Recommit to your marriage. Men, if you're saying, "She doesn't look like she did when we got married," have a look in your mirror. You're no prize yourself.

Recently I received a great thrill as I saw a sweet couple coming into church. They were holding hands. He was tall and trim, she was tall and thin, and if you could run the clock back fifty years, you would see a handsome young couple. I asked, "How are you this morning?"

He looked at me and with a big, deep voice said, "Pastor, we just celebrated our fifty-third wedding anniversary."

I said, "That's great, but listen to me. I want you to cut out holding hands here in church. That is a bad example for the teenagers!" They laughed, and I laughed, but I was thinking, *Thank God. There they are, fifty-three years together, still working on their marriage, still in love.* Friend, if a reproach you cannot blot out comes when you commit adultery, then there is an honor no one can steal away if you will stay committed to your spouse and stay faithful to the end.

Express brotherly kindness in addition to unconditional, covenant love in your marriage. Be a trustworthy spouse until Jesus takes you or your mate home.

THE DEMONSTRATION OF BROTHERLY KINDNESS WITH MONEY

Philadelphia—brotherly kindness. Be a person who shows brotherly kindness in ministry, in marriage, and finally, in money. In order to demonstrate brotherly kindness with our money, we must learn to be a contented Christian and a confident tither.

Learn to be content

Hebrews 13:5 says we are to let our character be free from the love of money. Remember, it is the *love* of money that is the root of all evil, not money itself. Don't fall in love with making money and do not be greedy with the money you make. Greed ruins many an individual. It ruined Achan in Joshua 7. He coveted and took a beautiful mantle, shiny silver, and gleaming gold, all items that were under the ban. It cost the nation of Israel a victory at Ai, and Achan his life. He, his entire family, and all his possessions were annihilated.

Greed got to Gehazi, Elisha's servant. After Naaman was healed of leprosy, Gehazi went back and tried to get some money from Naaman. Instead, Gehazi was struck with leprosy himself (2 Kings 5:27).

Acts 5 relates the greed of Ananias and Sapphira, the couple who lied to Peter and the apostles about their giving record. Their avarice caused Ananias to drop dead in the middle of a worship service, and the pallbearers were waiting at the door when Sapphira expired not long after.

Thirty pieces of silver destroyed Judas. Because of greed, he betrayed our Lord, and because of great guilt, he went out and hanged himself (Matthew 27:5).

The lesson here is that if you have money, don't be greedy with it. Conversely, if you don't have money, don't be covetous. We must all learn to be content with what we have. This does not mean we cannot pursue a competent living or strive to be the best we can be at what we do. But when the greed to have what someone else has causes you to covet, you have just broken the tenth commandment (Exodus 20:17).

BE CONTENT WITH WHAT YOU HAVE

When we answer the calling of sharing and strive to show brotherly kindness, we will strike the right balance with worldly goods. Jesus said it this way: "Seek first His kingdom and His righteousness; and all these things shall be added unto you" (Matthew 6:33).

We must also learn to be content right where we are. I take heart when I read what Paul wrote in Philippians 4:11. He had to *learn* to be content. It didn't come naturally, but supernaturally. In verse 13 he wrote, "I can do all things through Him who strengthens me." God made contentment possible for this apostle who spent so much of his life in jail.

This doesn't mean you can't have goals. It doesn't mean you do not have ambition. As my wife and I were talking about contentment not long back, I was reminded of the time when I had this very struggle in my own life. In the third year at our first church right out of seminary, I was becoming restless and unsure that I was in the place of ministry I wanted to be. As I saw it, my friends had moved up and moved on in the ministry. I felt I knew what God wanted me to do with my life and I didn't see how I could accomplish that where I was.

One day Liz looked at me and said, "If you don't get happy where you are, you're not going anywhere else." I got happy and stayed four more wonderful years! Be happy in today's circumstance and wait on the Lord for blessings tomorrow. God is not going to use you in a bigger and better way until you find happiness in Him. Wherever you are right now, I challenge you to learn to be content.

Over sixty years ago, Dr. George W. Truett was pastor of the First Baptist Church of Dallas, Texas. The church was about seven hundred members strong when he first arrived. Very quickly the church began to grow. During the years of his pastorate, Dr. Truett helped found Baylor Hospital in Dallas. He facilitated the recovery of Baylor University from bankruptcy. He started the Annuity Board of the Southern Baptist Convention. Truett was a master when it came to money management.

BE CONTENT WHERE YOU ARE

His friend, John D. Rockefeller, came to Dallas to visit. He heard Dr. Truett preach, and when he went back to Ohio he commissioned a group of people from the church where he was a member to go to Dallas and get Truett as their next pastor. Money was no object. They were to offer Dr. Truett any salary he desired. He could write his own ticket. (What a temptation!) After meeting with the men, Dr. Truett said he would come to Ohio on one condition—if they would move his congregation from Dallas to Ohio with him. The man who had out his wallet in anticipation, put it back when he saw money was not the issue. Dr. Truett was content right where he was. He stayed there for almost fifty years until he died and God took him home to heaven.

How is your level of contentment? Have you worked hard and managed well? Are you where God wants you to be?

Then learn to be content. Financially content people will demonstrate brotherly kindness to others.

Learn to be confident

Not only must we learn contentment, but we must also learn to be confident. Hebrews 13:5b-6 tells us that the Lord says,

> I will never desert you, nor will I ever forsake you, so that we confidently say, "The Lord is my helper, I will not be afraid. What shall man do to me?"

Note that these verses make it clear that we may say *with confidence* that we can trust in God. How do we learn this confidence? We learn confidence in God when we trust Him by tithing, by giving Him back a tenth of our income.

If you don't believe tithing is biblical, let me remind you that tithing is mentioned in the Bible even before the Law was given. In Genesis 14, Abraham laid at the feet of Melchizedek (identified in this passage as a "priest of God Most High") one-tenth of the spoils he collected as a result of his victory over Chedorlaomer and his allies. In Genesis 28:22, Jacob pledged to give God a tenth of all he was given. A tithe has always been God's plan for our giving.

GOD WILL PROVIDE IF YOU TRUST HIM

If you make a hundred dollars, give a tenth of it. If you make a million, give a tenth of it. If you make a billion, give a tenth. That is where you should start. Give your tithe to God's work through the local church. But know that you will never become a tither until you believe God will take care of your needs. In Malachi 3:10, God challenges us to test Him.

Tithe and He will provide those needs. You must learn to have confidence in Jehovah Jireh, our great provider God.

It is beyond imagination what God can do if you will trust Him. I find it hard to comprehend how God has blessed me so much in every area of my life. I went to a rural high school that did not teach any foreign languages. I attended a small community junior college, and managed to graduate from Samford University. I pulled a U-Haul full of all our possessions to Texas to seminary, and now I serve as the pastor of Olive Baptist Church. I know there is only one way I can explain it. *I serve a gigantic God.* He will take care of you if you will trust Him. As one of my laymen likes to remind me, "If we will take care of God's business, God will take care of our business." Amen!

THE EXAMPLE OF THE BROTHERLY KINDNESS OF CHRIST

Brotherly kindness—where do we get our example? To find the greatest illustration of brotherly kindness, look at the earthly ministry of Jesus. Jesus both taught and demonstrated the sharing of brotherly kindness. Matthew 4:23 tells us Jesus went throughout Galilee teaching and healing every kind of disease and sickness among the people.

In Matthew 14:14, Jesus felt compassion on the multitude because of all their needs and He healed their sick. Matthew 15:32 says that Jesus had compassion on the hungry multitude and fed four thousand people with seven loaves and a few small fish.

In Matthew 25:37, Jesus told us that in meeting the needs of any of His brothers who are hungry, thirsty, strangers, sick, or prisoners, it is the same as doing those things for Him.

In Mark 2:4, four men demonstrated brotherly kindness by bringing a paralytic to Jesus and letting him down through the roof to place him at Jesus' feet. Jesus healed the paralytic because of their faith and their actions.

Jesus showed compassion and brotherly love to countless lost and hurting people as He met their needs. He displayed God's love for suffering humanity again and again and again. As we grow in our Christian lives, we should strive to exemplify the brotherly kindness of Christ Jesus. Remember Hebrews 13:1? "Let love of the brethren continue." Let brotherly kindness—*philadelphia*—go on and on. Brotherly kindness must continue until Jesus comes again.

Share brotherly kindness in ministry to others, in your marriage to your spouse, and with your money in offerings to God. Exemplify the brotherly kindness of Christ and give what you have as Jesus has given to you. Express brotherly kindness as you answer the call to sharing.

REPEAT

1. Put the letter of each by the calling it matches:

_____ Faith	A. Service
_____ Moral Excellence	B. Submission
_____ Knowledge	C. Salvation
_____ Self-control	D. Sharing
_____ Perseverance	E. Sanctification
_____ Godliness	F. Suffering
_____ Brotherly Kindness	G. Separation

2. The final calling of God yet to come is ________________.

3. What is the meaning of *philadelphia?*

4. What are the three acts of brotherly kindness?

5. What are three areas in which we are to show brotherly kindness?

6. Two kinds of people we should minister to are ________________________ and the ________________________________.

7. What two things must we learn in regard to marriage?

8. Who provides the greatest example of brotherly kindness for us?

INTERPRET

9. Why should believers share brotherly kindness?

10. How does a man share brotherly kindness with his wife, and how does a wife show brotherly kindness to her husband?

11. How does tithing develop confidence in God?

12. How can one learn to become a tither? Can you expand on this beyond the comments made in this chapter?

PRACTICE

13. Name an unfamiliar person or one who is suffering who needs your sharing ministry. What do you plan to do for that person?

14. How do you plan to improve your level of contentment regarding your money?

15. If you are not a tither, what can you do to become one? Do you intend to do that?

PAUSE

Father, let brotherly kindness that glorifies You go on and on forever, and let it flourish in me. Teach me about brotherly kindness in my ministry, my marriage, and my money. Thank you for being the supreme example of brotherly kindness. Thank You for our opportunities to exemplify brotherly kindness to our neighbors and to strangers we meet. Thank You for the many acts of brotherly kindness shown to me, especially because they were done in Your precious name. Amen.

8
The Calling of *Spiritual Maturity*

Here is the question: is your scale complete? Or are you like a pianist sitting at a faulty piano banging on a key that will not produce the final tone to resolve the octave? Are you "almost complete" (an oxymoron, by the way), just walking around waiting for Jesus to come? We need the full orchestration of the Holy Spirit resounding in our hearts. As we begin with faith and continue to add the other callings to our lives, God will grow us up all the way to full spiritual maturity. In 2 Peter 1:5-7, the Bible says you start with

> IS YOUR SCALE COMPLETE?

FAITH, then you are to add
MORAL EXCELLENCE, to your moral excellence add
KNOWLEDGE, to your knowledge add
SELF-CONTROL, to your self-control add
PERSEVERANCE, to your perseverance add
GODLINESS, to your godliness add
BROTHERLY KINDNESS, and to your brotherly kindness add
LOVE.

As we look at the calling of love, we come to the completion of our journey through the eight callings of God. As our spiritual maturity evolves, we come to understand the genuine nature of *agape* love.

We must learn how to add to brotherly kindness this *agape* love found in 1 John 4:7-21.

> Beloved, let us love one another, for love is from God; and everyone who loves is born of God and knows God. The one who does not love does not know God, for God is love. We love, because He first loved us. If someone says, "I love God," and hates his brother, he is a liar; for the one who does not love his brother whom he has seen, cannot love God whom he has not seen. And this commandment we have from Him, that the one who loves God should love his brother also.

LOVE IS THE KEY TO SPIRITUAL MATURITY

A few years ago in a small town in Tennessee, there lived two men named Joe and Frank. Joe had a seventeen-year-old daughter who was a senior in high school. While sitting in his living room one evening, Joe's wife came in and said to him, "Our daughter has something to tell you."

His daughter sat down and said to him, "Daddy, this is the hardest thing I've ever had to say. It's bad."

"It doesn't matter how bad it is. You can tell me."

She looked at her dad and softly said, "I'm pregnant."

Joe jumped up, pointed his finger at his daughter, and shouted, "How dare you! How could you embarrass me like that in this town? We don't believe in having babies out of wedlock in this home. My good name will be ruined around here, so you can leave this house and never come back." She wept as she turned and walked away.

Frank lived across town and was a pastor of a local church. His own sixteen-year-old daughter shared the same announcement with him. The next Sunday, Frank stood behind his pulpit and said, "I want you to hear it from me before you hear it from anyone else. I have the permission of my daughter to tell you she is pregnant. We do not agree with what she has done, and she knows that. However, because she has come in repentance, we are going to treat her as the father in Scripture treated the prodigal son."

Which one of these fathers had the eighth note of spiritual maturity in his life? And can you guess which one of the two girls is still following Jesus today?

Agape love—the way God loves—is the mark of spiritual maturity. *Agape* love is more than just a sentimental emotion. Love (the emotional kind) is the most often used word and the most written about subject. We certainly sing about it more than anything else in the world.

At dinner one evening, I asked my wife and daughter to name all the songs they could think of with the word *love* in the title. They began to name song after song. I thought dinner was going to get cold.

Sadly, we so misunderstand God's love. God's *agape* love is the outgoing of the whole of one's being toward someone else for that person's benefit. The apostle John said we are lying if we declare that we love Christ whom we cannot see, and yet we do not love the people we do see (1 John 4:12a, 20). The person who truly loves God will love the individuals around him. We must love the people in our lives the way Jesus would have us love them. This is the mark of the mature believer.

The phrase "love is perfected" is found in both 1 John 4:12 and 4:17. Perfect love does not mean love without mistakes, but love that has come to maturity and to full completion. This perfect love brings us into harmony with the

Spirit of God. When this occurs, we love the way Jesus wants us to love—patterned, practiced, powerful and productive.

THE PATTERN OF PERFECT LOVE

The pattern of perfect love is found in 1 John 4:9-10.

> By this the love of God was manifested in us, that God has sent His only begotten Son into the world so that we might live through Him. In this is love, not that we loved God, but that He loved us and sent His Son to be the propitiation for our sins.

GOD GAVE US THE PATTERN FOR LOVE

Even while we did not love God, He loved us. He manifested His love to us, He showed us that love when he sent His Son to be our propitiation. Jesus paid the penalty for our sin. He appeased our debt. He showed us mercy. That is the pattern for perfect love. That word *propitiation* is the same word that is translated in Hebrews 9:5 as mercy seat.

In the Old Testament, we read about the ark of the covenant, Israel's most precious possession. The ark was a wooden chest covered in gold. Inside it were a gold jar of manna, two stone tablets containing the Ten Commandments written by God, and Aaron's staff. On two sides of the ark were carved cherubim, human-like statues with wings representing God's messengers. The golden lid, which symbolized the presence of God, was called the mercy seat. Once a year the high priest sprinkled the blood of a bull and a goat on the mercy seat as a symbol of payment for the sins of the Jewish nation.

When Jesus came, He became the propitiation—the appeasement for sin. On the day of atonement, He was the one whose blood-sprinkled body on the cross became the mercy seat at Calvary. He absorbed the entire wrath of God that should have been yours and mine. Jesus loved us so much that He paid our price. As His children, we are to love the same way. If we are going to love as Jesus loved, we will love *sacrificially*.

Jesus' love is an *unconditional* love. It is not based on our becoming better, but in fact, no matter how bad we are, Jesus loves us. I cannot fathom how God could love some of us when we are rascals to the core! His love is also *unmerited.* We can do nothing to earn it.

If we are not careful, we love with conditions, on the basis of merit, or as long as it doesn't cost us very much. We sometimes say, "If he pays me what he owes, then I'll love him" or "If she loves me back, I'll love her" or "If they would just change, I could love them." No, you love them in spite of who they are or what they have (or haven't) done. Isn't this what the Word of God calls us to do?

No doubt everyone has somebody who has tried to "crucify" him. But what was it our Lord said while He was on the cross? "Father, forgive them; for they do not know what they are doing" (Luke 23:34a). My problem comes when I have to pray, "Father, forgive them for they know *exactly* what they are doing." We are to love as Jesus loves. He is our pattern of perfect love.

It's difficult, isn't it? All of us can remember a time when someone hurt us deeply, when someone stuck a knife in your back and twisted it, as we used to say. That person doesn't deserve your love. But do you understand that you deserve none of God's love? Nevertheless, He lavished it on us. While we were still sinners, Christ died for us! That's the gospel. That's the *euaggelion*—the Good News. If we were perfect, we would not need loving. But we were lost, dead, damned, and doomed until He died for us. What a Savior! He has become the propitiation for us, the satisfaction of God's broken law. Even when we did not deserve it, did not merit it, and could not earn it, He loved us. Jesus is the pattern of perfect love.

THE PRACTICE OF PERFECT LOVE

Second, how do we practice perfect love? Notice 1 John 4:11-12.

> Beloved, if God so loved us, we also ought to love one another. No one has beheld God at any time; if we love one another, God abides in us, and His love is perfected in us.

Do you know how this world gets to know God? They get to know God by seeing Christ living in us and through us as we love this world. We find the descriptive outline for love in 1 Corinthians 13. Paul details the way love is supposed to be.

> Love is patient, love is kind, and is not jealous; love does not brag and is not arrogant, does not act unbecomingly; it does not seek its own, is not provoked, does not take into account a wrong suffered, does not rejoice in unrighteousness but rejoices with the truth; bears all things, believes all things, hopes all things, endures all things. Love never fails.

That is the New American Standard translation of these verses from the Greek. Read this same passage through the paraphrases of Eugene Peterson from *The Message*.

> Love never gives up. Love cares more for others than for self. Love doesn't want what it doesn't have. Love doesn't strut, doesn't have a swelled head, doesn't force itself on others, isn't always "me first," doesn't fly off the handle, doesn't keep score of the sins of others, doesn't revel when others grovel, takes pleasure in the flowering of truth, puts up with anything, trusts God always, always looks for the best, never looks back, but keeps going to the end.[7]

What a challenge! That kind of love seems impossible in the world we live in and with the kind of people we meet. It is so counterculture to what we see on television and movies and in print. But that is the love of God, and that *agape* love should be what we strive for in our own Christian walk toward spiritual maturity.

How do we get there? How do we practice love—the *agape* love of God? Simply put, we practice. Loving others will never become a regular habit in our lives until we repeat the action over and over. We should *practice* (verb) love until it becomes regular *practice* (noun). The proverbial phrase, "practice makes perfect" may not always be true, but in this case the practice of perfect love makes us more like Jesus.

We find a wonderful example in the life of Dr. E. Stanley Jones, considered by some to be the greatest Christian missionary since St. Paul. He spent most of his life as a missionary to the country of India. On one occasion after finishing a sermon on loving as Jesus loved, a pastor walked up to him and said, "Dr. Jones, I have practiced love. I have saturated my pastorate with love. I have loved my people. I have loved them and loved them and loved them! Still, I have one man in my church who is mean to me. He wants to split the church and he works against me. What should I do?" Dr. Jones looked at him and without blinking said, "Increase the dosage." The more opposition we face, the more we need to love. When people come against you—and they will—remember Dr. Jones' words and "increase the dosage." Keep on loving. Because God loved us so much, we must love one another.

THE POWER OF PERFECT LOVE

We have established the pattern and practice of perfect love. At this point you may be thinking (or screaming) "I can't do it! I can't love like that." I know you can't. And many times when we do try, we succeed only in being a failure. We fall and slip because we cannot do it ourselves. But God has given us the power of perfect love in 1 John 4:13.

> By this we know that we abide in Him and He in us, because He has given us of His Spirit.

The moment you are saved, the Spirit of Jesus lives in you and wants to live through you. He is the power to accomplish all that God asks of you. The art of love requires discipline, concentration, and patience. But most of all it requires the power of the Holy Spirit.

THE SPIRIT GIVES THE POWER OF PERFECT LOVE

I cannot love everyone. There are just some people who seem bent on making my life miserable. But when I die to myself and Jesus lives in me and His Spirit empowers me, He will love every person through me. I will then find myself loving others with the *agape* love of God more deeply than I could ever envision.

The power comes as I begin to accept and love people for who they are and where they are in life right now. I do not wait for them to change. *I* change. I say, "Holy Spirit, I can't love this person, but you can love him through me. I yield my feelings to your power." Then Jesus loves them through me.

There are kids today sitting in our churches who literally hate their parents. They cannot stand them. Those children will never be happy until they learn to love their parents as Jesus loves them. And there are parents who cannot stand their kids. They don't like them and wish they had never brought them into this world. It's too late. They are here, so parents better begin to accept their children just as they are. Surprise! That's when the power of the Spirit is released in your life.

I read a story of a psychologist who had a man come to him and say, "I have been married for twenty-two years, but I'm about to divorce my wife. She has gained weight and I do not like her anymore. She doesn't look like she used to look. She doesn't act like she used to act."

The psychologist said, "I have a plan for you. Here is what you do. For six weeks you treat her like a queen. You open every door and thank her for everything. You wash the dishes and take out the trash without her asking. You just care for her. Act like you love her. Then after six weeks, just as she has gotten used to you treating her so lovingly, tell her, 'I hate your guts' and walk out the door. I am telling you, it will kill her."

The husband said, "Man, that is a plan for me!"

He went home and followed the psychologist's instructions. He began to serve his wife.

In six weeks the psychologist called the man and asked, "Are you ready to sign the divorce papers?"

The husband replied, "Divorce? I'm married to the greatest woman in the world!"

What had happened? The husband's attitude had changed. He began to accept his wife and love her, and, of course, she had an attitude adjustment as well.

Christians, you are going to have to take a step with God toward people. Trust God to empower you to love that person you do not think you can love. And when you do, God will use it. He will use it in marvelous ways.

There was a man in my hometown who I hated, and my daddy hated him, too. He was our landlord and he was mean. He raised the rent on my daddy's store time and time again and threatened us with eviction. We didn't like him, and he did not like us. But God dealt with me and told me I had to go tell that man I loved him and ask his forgiveness for what I had said against him in our community.

I was sixteen and he was forty years old. It took me four days to get up the courage, but I finally went into his store. I extended my hand, called his name, and said, "Sir, in Jesus' name, forgive me. I love you." I could never have done that on my own. I had to be close to God for that to happen. I had prayed, I had yielded, and I had asked for the power of the Spirit. He loved through me. I learned that if we will die to self, find the principle of God, stand therein, and go forward, God will reward our efforts.

Dr. Jerry Vines tells this story of a man in his church in Rome, Georgia. Dr. Vines says, "I had to confess that was the best-smelling man I had ever smelled in all my life. Every time he would come by, he just smelled so good. Finally I stopped him one day and said, 'Sir, what cologne are you wearing? I mean, you just smell so pleasant every time you walk by.'

"He said, 'I work in a wholesale floral shop and handle roses all day long. I get that stuff on me and I just can't get it off. You know, if you hang around roses long enough, you begin to smell like them.'"

Dr. Vines said, "I jotted that down and, you know, if you hang around Jesus you will begin to have a sweet aroma just like Him. When you hang around Jesus you have the smell of grace about you."

THE PRODUCT OF PERFECT LOVE

The pattern, the practice, and the power of perfect love are followed by what I call the product of perfect love. What will this kind of love produce? The answer is in 1 John 4:17.

> By this, love is perfected with us, that we may have confidence in the day of judgment; because as He is, so also are we in this world.

Perfect love yields confidence in the day of judgment. There is no fear in love. When we begin to love as Jesus loves, it brings fearlessness in the face of judgment along with a freedom to love others.

> LOVING AS JESUS LOVES GIVES CONFIDENCE FOR THE DAY OF JUDGMENT

On that day of judgment, if you are lost, have never trusted in Christ as your Savior, you will stand at the Great White Throne and then be cast into outer darkness.

If you are a believer, you will stand at the judgment seat of God and give an account for everything that you have done (Romans 14:10, 12). You will give an account for showing love or showing hatred. This judgment will not cause you to lose entrance into heaven, but it will cost you in reward and stature in the culture of eternity.

Are you thinking something like this: "If I died or Jesus were to come, I am scared to death that heaven would not be my home"? If so, you can live without that fear. When you begin to find the love of God and then practice the love of God, it causes a fearlessness in your life that provides confidence that you will belong to God in the judgment. Why? Because when you are showing the Christ-life in this world through love, it lends a confidence for the judgment of the life that is to come.

Not only is there confidence in the day of judgment, but there is a confidence about life in this world. Read 1 John 4:17b again: "…because as He is, so are we in this world." The product of His perfect love—confidence—gives us the power to live free from fear in our day-to-day lives. Second Timothy 1:7 says,

> For God has not given us a spirit of timidity,
> but of power and love and discipline.

Love—it is God's way.

THE PROOF OF PERFECT LOVE

The manifestations of *agape* love give proof that perfect love is in our lives. I want to delineate four markers that corroborate the presence of perfect love.

That love is:

- **Active**
- **Transitive**
- **Serving**
- **Sacrificing**

First, *perfect love is active.* It demands expression. You cannot say, "I'm going to love" and then sit back and never show it. If you are going to love your spouse, your children, your grandkids, your church, and if you are going to love your God, your love must be active.

Second, *perfect love is transitive.* It requires an object. There must be something or someone to receive your love. If you are going to love, you have to present it to an individual, to a cause, or toward some object.

LOVE MUST HAVE AN OBJECT

Third, *perfect love is serving.* Remember the call to service in chapter four? That is all about love.

Fourth and finally, *perfect love is sacrificing.*

Every Friday my administrative assistant places my schedule in the front of my Bible detailing where I am going and what I am going to do every day of the upcoming week. One particular Friday I looked down at my list and there was a name of a person I was scheduled to see at 4 p.m. that very day—the last thing to finish my week. Now, I like to finish well. I don't like some difficult and stressful meeting to end the work week, so I asked her, "Who is this? I don't know this person."

She replied, "Trust me. This will be good."

At 4 p.m. the man walked into my office. He was carrying a bucket. I thought, *What? Are we going out to the Widow's Garden to pick peas?* He began to tell me about his life and how God had changed him. He told me how our church had ministered to him and to his family.

He said, "Pastor, I've come to make a request." I said, "Yes, sir."

He said, "A few weeks ago you preached about Jesus washing feet as a servant, and I have come to ask if I can wash my pastor's feet."

That man went to the restroom next to my office and filled his bucket with water. He then took off my shoes and socks. He held my feet like they were pieces of porcelain. He took a little bar of soap, lathered his hands, and while he washed my feet he prayed for me. He thanked God for me. He prayed for my wife and my children and for our dear church. When he finished, he took a towel and dried my feet. As I sat in my chair he crawled up in my lap, a man old enough to be my father, and hugged me around the neck. And I thought, *Dear God, I have seen the eighth note of the octave.*

How can you say that you love God and hate anybody? The Bible says you are a liar if you say you love God and hate your neighbor. I have good news for you. No matter how mean your heart feels, Jesus loves you. You see, I could have said to that man, "No, sir, I'm not going to allow you to wash my feet." I had to receive his sacrificial act of love. Jesus loves you but you have to receive that love by faith. When you do, He will change your life and set you on the road to loving those who are all around you.

God showed His *agape* love toward us when Jesus became the propitiation for our sins—not only for our sins, but also for the sins of the whole world. Jesus went to the cross. He was pierced, He was nailed, He bled, and He died because He loved you. They took Him down off that cross and placed His body in a borrowed tomb. Then three days later angels moved the stone away and He arose for you. Today He sits at the right hand of the Father where He is praying for you. One day when the horn blows and the heavenly shout is heard, He will come back. Is He coming back for you?

BRING YOUR LIFE INTO HARMONY WITH GOD

I am known for many things, but having a great singing voice is not one of them. As a matter of fact, the sound engineer at our church cuts off my microphone just as soon as he sees me start to sing.

I expect my singing ability will be greatly enhanced when I get to heaven. But I'm not so sure that any of us will be able to sing in that heavenly choir without some practice. We must learn to bring our lives into harmony with God's will here on earth.

Does the trumpet player join the orchestra without having first learned the musical skills necessary to harmonize with the rest of the musicians? Certainly not. As we gain instruction through the Word and practice that instruction through these eight callings of God, we will reach spiritual maturity and our lives become in tune with heaven's song. By God's grace we are made ready to sing.

OUR OCTAVE IS COMPLETE WITH THE CALLING OF LOVE

> And I heard, as it were, the voice of a great multitude and as the sound of many waters and as the sound of mighty peals of thunder, saying, Hallelujah! For the Lord our God, the Almighty reigns.
>
> Revelation 19:6-7

REPEAT

List the calling of God for each of these attributes they develop.

____
which is the call to salvation

____
which is the call to separation

____
which is the call to sanctification

____
which is the call to service

____
which is the call to suffering

____
which is the call to submission

____
which is the call to sharing

____
which is the call to spiritual maturity

2. What is *agape* love?

3. In what Scripture passage is the pattern of perfect love found?

4. What are two words that describe the way Jesus loved?

5. List at least four characteristics of love found in 1 Corinthians 13.

6. What are three requirements for developing the art of love?

7. Where do we get the power to love as Jesus loved?

8. There are four markers that corroborate the presence of perfect love. Love is:
   ______________________, ______________________,
   ______________________, ______________________.

INTERPRET

9. How can you develop love for a person who is unlovable?

10. What happens when we practice a loving attitude toward an unloving person?

11. How does the way we love prepare us for the judgment to come?

12. What effect will failure to learn to love like Jesus loved—never developing spiritual maturity—have on your eternal life in heaven?

PRACTICE

13. Whom have you not treated with love that you are now going to love through the Spirit's power? How do you plan to do this?

14. If there is someone whose forgiveness you need for treating them in an unloving way, what do you plan to do about it, and when?

PAUSE

Father, I thank You that You have loved me. I thank You that You sent Your Son to die for me. Lord, I pray that I will take Your pattern and make it my practice to love others. I ask that You grant me Your power to love as You have loved. Have Your way in my life always. In Jesus' name I pray, Amen.

BIBLE STUDY HELPS

PERSONAL BIBLES
(may include any or all of the following)

- Articles on how to study the Bible
- A plan for reading the Bible through in one year or two years
- A Harmony of the Gospels
- Lists of the parables of Jesus
- Lists of the miracles of Jesus
- A pronunciation guide
- A concordance alphabetically listing names, places, and topics mentioned in the Bible with brief explanations and a list of references concerning the entries
- Maps of Bible lands from different historic periods
- References down the center or at the bottom of each page indicating other scriptures relating to the noted item
- Information preceding each book that includes information on the date and place of writing, author, historical background, and a survey of its contents

ADDITIONAL BIBLE STUDY HELPS
(may be found in books and/or computer programs)

- Commentaries that contain verse-by-verse interpretation and explanation
- Bible dictionaries containing definitions and identities of biblical words, names, places, events, etc.
- Concordances, larger and more complete than those in personal Bibles
- Study Bibles with articles on history, biography, culture, geography, theology, statistics, and tables interspersed throughout the text. In addition there may be appendices of thematic listings for specific studies.
- Bible atlases with information on periods and geographical areas of Bible history and locations
- Bible study books designed to offer in-depth instruction of a specific book of the Bible.

END NOTES

Chapter Three

1. http:/www.theologicalstudies.org

2. http://en.wikipedia.org/wiki/List_of_best-selling_books

3. http://en.wikipedia.org/wiki/Bible_translations

4. http://en.wikipedia.org/wiki/Modern_English_Bible _translations

5. Josh McDowell, *The New Evidence That Demands a Verdict* (Nashville: Thomas Nelson Publishers, 1999), 4-6.

Chapter Five

6. http://www.winstonchurchill.org/speeches /speeches-of-winston-churchill/1941-1945-war-leader

Chapter Eight

7. Eugene H. Peterson, *The Message* (Colorado Springs, CO: Navpress, 2003)